Back to Basics: Debt Management

by Steve Bucci, BA, MA and Mary Reed

WILEY

Publisher's Acknowledgments

Senior Acquisitions Editor:
Tracy Boggier

Project Manager:
Chad R. Sievers

Compilation Editor:
Georgette Beatty

Technical Editor:
Maria Erickson, CFP, MBA

Production Editor:
G. Vasanth Koilraj

Cover Images: (shredder)
© Natallashein / Getty Images,
(wallet) © LokFung / Getty Images

Cover Design: Wiley

Back to Basics: Debt Management

Published by John Wiley & Sons, Inc.
111 River St.
Hoboken, NJ 07030-5774
http://www.wiley.com

For general information on our other products and services, please contact our Business Development
Department in the U.S. at 317-572-3205.

ISBN 978-1-119-47282-7 (pbk); ISBN 978-1-119-47281-0 (ePub); ISBN 978-1-119-47285-8 (ePDF)

Manufactured in the United States of America

F10009826 050319

Contents

1

Assessing Where You Are Financially

You've bought this book, so you're probably at least a little worried — maybe *really* worried — about your financial health. Perhaps your debts have you biting your nails, and you're not sure what to do about them. And you probably don't have a good handle on the true state of your finances. After all, it's human nature to try to avoid bad news.

Facing financial facts can be unsettling and even scary. When you know the state of your finances, it becomes hard to ignore the fact that improving your financial situation requires changing your lifestyle and making some big sacrifices. But no matter how scary it is, confronting the reality of your financial situation is *essential* — and the good news is that seeking out this book is a terrific first step to doing just that.

This chapter begins your next step: figuring out where you are so you know where you need to go. Until you come face to face with the actual facts of your finances, you may find it impossible to develop the resolve and self-discipline you need to implement your plan of action. That's why the chapter begins with a series of fact-finding exercises to get you going.

The more bad news you get as you complete these exercises, the more critical it is that you get serious about dealing with your debts. The sooner you do that, the quicker and easier it will be to improve your finances and the less likely it will be that your creditors will take some of your assets or that you'll have to file for bankruptcy.

Some Preliminary Questions

You can get a rough sense of your debt problem by honestly answering the following questions. The more "yes" answers, the more work you have to do:

- Are you clueless about how much you owe your creditors?
- Over time, is a growing percentage of your household income going toward paying your debts?

_____

_____

_____

- Do you ever pay your bills late because you don't have enough money?
- Have you stopped paying some of your debts?
- Are you paying only the minimum due on some of your credit cards because you can't afford to pay more?
- Are you using credit and/or credit card cash advances to help pay debts and/or your basic living expenses, such as groceries, rent, or utilities?
- Have you maxed out any of your credit cards, or have any of your cards been canceled for nonpayment?
- Do you have little or nothing in savings?
- Have you borrowed money from friends or relatives to pay your bills?
- Have debt collectors begun calling you, and/or are you receiving threatening notices from some of your creditors?
- Are you having a hard time concentrating at work because you are worried about money?
- Are you losing sleep because of your finances?

_____

_____

_____

- Have you and your spouse or partner begun to fight about money?
- Are you drinking more or using drugs to try to cope with your money worries?

Your Relationship with Money

You may have the misconception that you are what you buy. You may believe on some level that the more you spend, the more successful and important you are. Developing that mindset is easy because everyone is bombarded with messages that equate money and stuff with success. How often do you see ads promoting frugality, saving, or self-denial? If you're struggling to keep up with the Joneses, you may need to reevaluate your friendships. The Joneses may be driving you straight to the poorhouse.

Recognize emotional spending

Maybe you spend money for emotional reasons. For example, think about what you do when you feel sad or disappointed, or when you want to celebrate a success. Do you head to

---

---

the mall? Do you click on your favorite retail website? Do you treat yourself to an expensive meal or enjoy a weekend getaway even though you really can't afford it? If so, spending may have become a sort of addiction. Everyone likes a reward from time to time, but doing so continually is a problem, and losing track of whether you can afford to treat yourself is a cause for real concern.

If emotional spending describes your behavior to a T, you need to get a handle on it fast. One option is to meet with a mental health professional; you may qualify for help from a low-cost/no-cost clinic in your area. Or get involved with Debtors Anonymous (www. debtorsanonymous.org or 781-453-2743). DA uses the time-tested methods of Alcoholics Anonymous to help people understand why they spend and gain control over their spending.

Live for the moment

Maybe your problem is that you "live for today" and don't think about tomorrow. In some ways, living in the moment is great, sure — but not if you turn a blind eye toward your future.

_____

_____

_____

How do you know if you've got this attitude toward money? You probably

- Use credit too much.
- Don't try to pay off your credit balances as quickly as possible, telling yourself there will be plenty of time to do that later.
- Save little, if anything.
- Rarely, if ever, take time to look online at your bank accounts, keep a close eye on your credit reports and credit score, or pay attention to credit card statement details and what you've spent money on.

Such attitudes are self-destructive and catch up with you eventually. You're reading this book, so they may already have.

Check Your Credit Reports

Three national credit-reporting companies operate in the United States: Equifax, Experian, and TransUnion. Reviewing the information in your credit report from each company is an excellent way to see your true financial picture.

_____

_____

_____

Get copies of your credit reports

For a comprehensive survey of your creditworthiness, order a copy of your credit report from each of the national credit-reporting agencies, not just from one. Each report may contain slightly different information about you, partly because not all creditors report all consumer account payment information to all three agencies.

 You are entitled to one free copy of each of your credit reports every year. To order yours, go to www.annual creditreport.com.

If you've already obtained free copies of your credit reports during the past 12 months, you must pay a fee to order additional copies. In most states, the cost is $10 per report (and some states also charge a sales tax), although the cost is less in some states. You can call your state attorney general's office to find out.

Also, you are always entitled to a free credit report if

- You are unemployed and intend to apply for a job within 60 days.
- You are receiving public welfare assistance.

- You believe that you have been the victim of identity theft or fraud.
- You have been denied credit, employment, insurance, or a place to rent within the past 60 days because of information in your credit report.

To order additional copies of your credit reports after you've obtained your free annual ones, you must contact each of the three credit-reporting agencies individually:

- **Equifax:** www.equifax.com/personal/
- **Experian:** www.experian.com
- **TransUnion:** www.transunion.com

If you order additional copies by mail, put your request in a letter that includes the following information, and be sure to sign it:

- Your full name (including Jr., Sr., III, and so on)
- Your Social Security number
- Your date of birth
- Your current address and previous addresses for the past five years
- Your phone number, including area code
- The name of your current employer

Why your reports matter

The credit report you get is the same one that your current creditors and potential future creditors use to make decisions about you. The more negative information that is in your credit histories (such as past-due accounts, accounts in collection, accounts that your creditors have charged off as uncollectible, tax liens, and so on), the worse your finances are.

Your existing creditors may use the information to decide whether to raise the interest rates you are paying, lower your credit limits, or even cancel your credit. And whenever you apply for new credit, the creditors review your credit record information to decide whether to approve your application, how much credit to give to you, the interest rate you must pay, and so on.

Many insurance companies, landlords, and employers also review your credit record information. If they find a lot of negative information, insurance companies may not agree to insure you or may charge you higher-than-normal premiums; landlords may refuse to rent to you; and employers may not want to hire you or to give you the promotion you applied for.

The federal Fair Credit Reporting Act says that most negative information remains in your credit reports for 7½ years and that a Chapter 7 liquidation bankruptcy and a Chapter 13 reorganization of debt linger there for ten years. However, the three credit-reporting agencies have a policy of reporting completed Chapter 13s for only seven years. A tax lien sticks around until you pay it.

Your FICO Score

A growing number of creditors, as well as insurance companies, employers, and landlords, use something called a FICO score together with (or even instead of) your credit history to make decisions about you. Your FICO score is a numeric representation of your creditworthiness and is derived from your credit history information. Like your credit history, the score is a snapshot of how you've managed credit in the past. As such, your FICO score is generally considered an indicator of how well you are likely to manage credit in the future.

Actually, a variety of different credit scores exist. Equifax, Experian, and TransUnion have developed their own credit scores. (Each credit-reporting agency sells its credit score on its website.) But the FICO score has become the industry standard. You can order your FICO score by going to www.myfico.com.

Your FICO score can range from 300 to 850. The higher, the better: A score of at least 720 is considered to be very good. If your score is well below 720, you may still qualify for credit from some creditors, but you'll be charged a higher interest rate and you may not qualify for as much credit as you would like. Likewise, insurance companies may be willing to sell you insurance, but you'll probably pay extra for the coverage and you may not be able to purchase as much insurance as you would like. When you have a low FICO score, some landlords will not rent to you, and you may not qualify for certain kinds of jobs, especially those that involve handling money.

 You can raise your FICO score by improving the state of your finances. For example, your credit score will go up if you

- Pay down your account balances.
- Begin paying your bills or debts on time.
- Build up your savings.
- Minimize the amount of credit you apply for.
- Correct problems in your credit histories.

Spending versus Income

Now comes the *real* measure of the state of your finances: figuring out how your total spending compares to your total household income.

The necessary materials

To complete this exercise, you need a pad of paper, a pen or pencil, and a calculator. You also need the following financial information:

- Check registers or online access to your checking account
- Bank statements
- Receipts for major purchases not made with a credit card
- Credit card account statements
- Other expense records for the past 12 months

You also need records of your income for the past 12 months, such as pay stubs and deposit slips or direct deposit information. If you're self-employed, you need your business records.

Your spouse or partner should gather the same information because the goal of this exercise is to give you as complete a picture as possible of how your *household* spending compares to your *household* income.

Categorize your expenses

Creating a worksheet modeled after the one in Table 1-1 (at the end of this section) will help you organize your spending and income information and make sure that you don't overlook anything. This worksheet will also come in handy in Chapter 4, where you build a budget.

The worksheet in Table 1-1 divides your spending into three categories:

- **Fixed expenses:** These expenses stay the same from month to month. Examples are your rent or mortgage, car loan, home equity loan, and insurance.

- **Variable expenses:** These expenses tend to vary from month to month. Examples are your groceries, gas, utilities, restaurant meals, movies, music, and books.

- **Periodic expenses:** These expenses may be fixed or variable. You pay them just once in a while, such as quarterly, every six months, or annually. Tuition, some kinds of insurance, property taxes, and dues are examples.

Some expenses listed as *fixed* on the worksheet may actually be *periodic* expenses for you. For example, instead of paying your auto insurance every month, you may pay it every quarter.

After you've calculated total annual amounts for each of your debts and for all your living expenses, enter them on the appropriate worksheet lines.

Figure out the fritter factor

It's *so* easy to fritter money away, isn't it? A latte here, a happy-hour drink or two there, lunch out with friends or colleagues, new clothes. Before you know it, it's the end of the month and you don't have any money left. Where did it all go? Most likely, you unconsciously frittered it away on unnecessary, miscellaneous items. Each purchase may not have cost much, but together over a month's time, frittering adds up to a significant amount. How much?

Say that every workday you spend $3 on a latte. In a month, you spend $60, and in a year that small daily purchase adds up to $720. If you also spend $2.50 per day for a bagel or pastry to go with the latte, you're spending $110 each month and more than $1,300 per year.

If you're like the vast majority of people, you get paid money much less often than you spend it. You probably get paid every week, every two weeks, or every month — but you spend money every day. This leads to a distortion in how you think about money and makes frittering all too easy.

To help you get a handle on how much you fritter away, for one month write down *everything* you purchase with cash, a debit card, or a credit card. Your spouse or partner should do the same. Carry a small notebook with you whenever you leave the house so you can record every expenditure right away instead of trying to remember it later. When the month is up, add up everything you spent on nonessential items. You may be shocked to see how much it amounts to. Multiply this number by 12, and put that number in your worksheet under "Other" in the "Variable Spending" section.

Total spending and earnings

Add up the numbers in each of the three spending categories in Table 1-1 to get a subtotal for each category. Then add up the subtotals. The final number represents the amount you are currently spending each year.

Next, add up all the income you received during the same 12-month period. Take into account not just your net household income (your *take-home pay*, which is gross income minus all deductions including taxes), but also any other income you or your spouse or partner may receive: government benefits, investments, royalties, child support or spousal support, income from a family business, and so on. Record that total on your worksheet.

If you are entitled to child support and/or spousal support but the payments rarely come, don't include those amounts when you calculate total annual income for your household. If it's unreliable income, you can't count on it to help cover your spending.

Calculate your financial bottom line

When you have a total annual income amount and a total annual spending amount, subtract your spending total from your income total.

If the final number you calculate is negative, you can probably guess what that means: The amount you are spending is more than your annual household income. You may be financing your lifestyle by using credit cards and cash advances, and/or you may be falling behind on some of your obligations. Furthermore, you may not be paying some of your bills at all, which means that if you add the amount of those bills into your calculations, you have an even bigger deficit.

If you ended up with a positive number, your finances may be in better shape than you think — or not. Showing a positive number but not having savings or little extra money in your checking account is a red flag that you probably missed something. If the number is small, you may be just barely staying ahead. And if your bottom line is positive only because you're paying just the minimum due on your credit cards each month or because you've stopped paying some of your debts, you have no cause for celebration. If this describes your situation, you are treading water, at best, and a financial setback such as a job loss or expensive illness could be devastating.

Annual Income	
Your household take-home pay	$_____
Child support income	$_____
Alimony income	$_____
Other income (specify the source)	$_____
Other income (specify the source)	$_____
Other income (specify the source)	$_____
Total Annual Income	$_____
Annual Spending	
Fixed Spending	
Rent	$_____
Mortgage	$_____
Home equity loan	$_____
Condo or homeowner's association fee	$_____
Car payment	$_____
Other loans	$_____
Homeowner's insurance	$_____
Renter's insurance	$_____
Health insurance	$_____
Auto insurance	$_____
Life insurance	$_____
Other insurance	$_____
Childcare	$_____
Dues and fees	$_____

Table 1-1: *Annual Income and Spending Worksheet*

Fixed Spending	
Cable/satellite service	$_____
Internet access	$_____
Child support obligation	$_____
Alimony obligation	$_____
Other fixed expenses (specify type)	$_____
Other fixed expenses (specify type)	$_____
Other fixed expenses (specify type)	$_____
Other fixed expenses (specify type)	$_____
Total Annual Fixed Spending	$_____
Variable Spending	
Groceries	$_____
Cigarettes	$_____
Alcohol	$_____
Utilities	$_____
Cellphone	$_____
Gas for car	$_____
Public transportation	$_____
Tolls and parking	$_____
Newspapers, books, and magazines	$_____
Allowances	$_____
After-school activities for kids	$_____
Babysitting	$_____
Entertainment	$_____
Restaurant meals	$_____

(continued)

Variable Spending	
Personal care products	$_____
Clothing	$_____
Body care (haircuts, manicures, massages)	$_____
Laundry and dry cleaning	$_____
Out-of-pocket medical expenses	$_____
Lawn care	$_____
Home repair and maintenance	$_____
Other (specify type)	$_____
Other (specify type)	$_____
Other (specify type)	$_____
Other (specify type)	$_____
Total Annual Variable Spending	$_____
Periodic Spending	
Insurance	$_____
Auto registration and inspection	$_____
Subscriptions	$_____
Charitable donations	$_____
Tuition	$_____
Dues and fees	$_____
Income taxes	$_____
Property taxes	$_____
Other (specify type)	$_____
Other (specify type)	$_____

Table 1-1 *(continued)*

Periodic Spending	
Other (specify type)	$_____
Other (specify type)	$_____
Total Annual Periodic Spending	$_____
Total Annual Spending	$_____
Total Annual Income	$_____
minus	–
Total Annual Spending	$_____
equals	=
Your Bottom Line	$_____

Assess Spending Habits

Congratulations! You just took the most important step on the road to financial recovery. To varying degrees, everyone lives in a self-imposed fog when it comes to spending money. Spending becomes a comfortable habit — just the way you go about your daily life — and habits are always hard to break. But you're on your way. Now that you've committed yourself to recovery, you can take a closer look at where your money is going, consider the possibility that overspending is a habit, and, if it is, examine ways to deal with it.

_____

_____

_____

Documenting your expenses has proven the obvious: You've wasted money and probably made some lousy financial decisions. Who hasn't? (If you haven't assessed your spending habits, see the earlier section "Spending versus Income.") Now that you have a handle on the problem, you're in position to take control. With the right attitude, eliminating unnecessary expenditures can be a little like a treasure hunt. There's extra money out there — you just have to find it.

No one can tell you how much to spend on any particular item — that's your call — but here are a few things to zero in on:

- **Credit card payments:** If a big chunk of your monthly income is going to pay credit card bills (especially if you're paying minimum payments), bankruptcy may be the best solution by far (see Chapter 8). If this is the case, you're just spinning your wheels in the worst of all worlds — paying interest without significantly reducing the principal amount of the debts. For example, say you've got a fairly modest credit card debt of $3,000. At 17 percent interest — and a lot of times the interest rate is even higher — you'll be indebted to the credit card company for about 35 years if you just make minimum payments.

- **Daily dribbles:** Everyone lives their lives amid daily patterns that eventually become habits. Many times, these habits include unnecessary spending that provides no real benefit or enjoyment. What seems like small stuff eventually adds up. Again, consider the latte on the way to work, the buck you put in the soda machine, and the $2.50 you spend for an afternoon snack — all without even thinking about it. Over the course of a year, you've blown $1,430. If you invested this money for 20 years at 10 percent interest, you'd end up with more than $80,000.

- **Extravagances:** True, one person's luxury is another's necessity, but you really need to think long and hard before plopping down $100 at a restaurant, regularly upgrading to the latest and greatest phone, or $60 for a pay-per-view prize fight on TV. It's sometimes helpful — though painful — to figure out how much work you had to do to pay for a particular treat. If a night on the town costs you a day and a half of work, is it really a good return on your investment?

- **Impulse purchases:** In the later section "Catalog What You Own," you're asked to list all your belongings; for now, just make a trip to your attic, basement, and garage. If you're like most people, you'll see tons of stuff you've bought but rarely, if ever, use. Simplify. And go further: Sell.

- **Gifts:** Studies show that many folks spend lavishly on gifts they would never buy for themselves. Christmas, of course, is the granddaddy of budget-busters. Scale back gifting.

- **Overwhelming mortgage payments:** If you obtained your mortgage recently, most of your monthly payment goes toward the interest. You may not have much equity, and the home may not be worth keeping — especially if it's a second mortgage.

- **Car payments:** If you're struggling to maintain payments on a new car, you may want to consider selling it and buying something more affordable. Plenty of reliable, moderately priced used cars are on the market.

Catalog What You Own

When you know what your spending habits and your earnings are, you need to get an equally firm grasp on what you *own*. Documenting your assets

- Helps determine what property you may lose by filing bankruptcy.

- Lets you know whether selling things could head off bankruptcy.

- Demonstrates how little you have to show for credit card debt.

Use Table 1-2 to get a rough idea of what you own and how much it's worth.

Asset	Value
Real Property	
Your home	
Other real property	
Timeshares	
Motor Vehicles	
Bank Account Balances	
Household Goods	
Furniture	
Appliances	
Audio and video equipment	
Computers and accessories	
Other household items	

Table 1-2: *What You Own*

(continued)

Asset	Value
Art Objects and Collectibles	
Jewelry	
Firearms	
Hobby Equipment	
Stocks, Bonds, and Other Investments	
Cash Value of Life Insurance	
Interests in Any Trusts	
Business Interests and Inventory	
Money You Are Owed	
Alimony and support	
Bonuses at work	
Accounts receivable	
Claims where you can sue someone	
Commissions	
Tax refunds	
Money You Are Entitled to Because Someone Died	
Life insurance	
Distributions from an estate	
Patents and Copyrights	
Tools and Machinery Used for Work	
Cash Value of Pensions	
Office Equipment Not Included in Household Goods	
Other Assets	

Table 1-2 *(continued)*

Add Up What You Owe

Purveyors of consumer credit want you to think in terms of monthly payments instead of considering the total amount you owe. It's a lot easier to sell that new car when the customer focuses on a $400 monthly payment rather than on a $25,000 albatross. But when it comes to assessing your financial condition, knowing the total amount of your debts is critical.

Consider home and car loans separately from other debts, for two reasons:

- You can reduce or eliminate these loans if you sell the house or car.
- Bankruptcy affects home and car loans differently than other debts.

You can find out how much you owe on these loans by phoning the creditor. If you're behind in payments, also find out how much it will take to bring the loan *current* (that is, not behind anymore, as opposed to paid in full).

Filling the blanks in Table 1-3 helps you get a grip on what you owe.

	Total Balance Owed	Monthly Payment	Value of Home/Car	Arrearage (Amount You're Behind)
Residence				
Other real estate				
Cars				

Table 1-3: *What You Owe on Mortgage and Car Loans*

Calculating how much you owe on other debts is a little tougher. Ordering credit reports is one place to start (covered earlier in this chapter and in Chapter 3). You can often determine the amounts owed on judgments, child support, alimony, fines, and restitution obligations from documents on file in the courthouse. You can get a rough idea of how much you owe on income taxes by looking at copies of your income tax returns, but this method doesn't give you the amount of penalties and interest that have accrued. Hopefully, you have a rough idea of how much you owe on student loans. If not, find out.

After you know what you owe, use Table 1-4 to help you keep track of it.

If creditors don't know where you live, or have given up on you, don't ring their bell by calling them. However, you may have to face the music about the money that you owe eventually because some types of debts will not go away.

So use the time when creditors are not hounding you to plan how you will deal with your debts. Among other options, for example, you can try to increase your income and/or save more money so that you can eventually contact your creditors and offer to satisfy your debts by paying a percentage of their total amounts. You can also contact a reputable credit-counseling organization for help working out payment plans with your creditors, or you can look into bankruptcy as a possible solution to your financial problems.

Type of Debt	Total Amount Owed
Judgments	
Income taxes	
Child support and alimony	
Student loans	
Fines and restitution obligations	
Medical bills	
Credit card balances	
Loans to friends and relatives	

Table 1-4: *How Much Do You Owe on Other Debts?*

2

How Credit Works

Credit is a powerful tool. Unfortunately, it can also bury you if you use it improperly. The subject generally isn't well taught in schools or, for that matter, in the family. If you know the rules of the credit game, you stand a much better chance of getting a good score. Everyone makes mistakes, but what's important is knowing how to recover from your mistakes without compounding the damage.

Consider this chapter your jumping-off point to the world of credit. The goal is to make your credit the best it can be and keep it that way — not just for the sake of having good credit, but so you can live the American Dream of having a decent job, a place to call home, and whatever else you desire.

What Credit Is

Credit has its origins in the Latin word *credo,* which means "I believe." These considerations are the real underlying issues of credit: Do you do what you promise? Are you believable and trustworthy? Have you worked hard to build a good reputation? Little is more precious to a person than being trusted — and that's what credit is all about.

You can also define credit as follows:

- Recognition given for some action or quality; a source of pride or honor; trustworthiness; credibility

- Permission for a customer to have goods or services that will be paid for at a later date

- The reputation of a person or firm for paying bills or other financial obligations

The concept of credit is simple: You receive something *now* in return for your promise to pay for it *later.* Credit doesn't increase your income. It allows you to conveniently spend money that you've already saved — or to spend the money today that you know you'll earn tomorrow.

Because businesses can make more money when you use credit, they encourage you to use it as often as possible. For creditors to make as much money as possible, they want you to spend as much as you can, as fast as you can. Helping you spend your future earnings today is their basic plan. This plan may make them very happy — but it may not do the same for you.

Consumers can avail themselves of many types of credit today, which is no surprise to you. But despite the endless variations and terms that seem to exist, most credit can be classified as one of two major types:

- **Secured credit:** As the name implies, *security* is involved — that is, the lender has some protection if you default on the loan. Your secured loan is backed by property, not just your word. House mortgages and car loans fall into this category. Generally, the interest rates for secured credit are lower and the *term* (the length of time before you have to pay it all off) may be longer because the risk of loss is lessened by the lender's ability to take whatever you put up for security.

_____

_____

_____

• **Unsecured credit:** This type of credit is usually more expensive, shorter term, and considered a higher risk by the lender. Because it is backed by your promise to repay it — but not by an asset — lenders are more vulnerable if you default. Most credit cards fall into this category.

Chances are you've always looked at credit from your own perspective, the viewpoint of the *borrower*. From where you're standing, you may be the customer who should be catered to. Consumer spending is two-thirds of the U.S. economy, and much of that is generated using lines of credit or credit cards. Whether you use credit as a convenience or because you need to spread out your payments, you keep the economy humming and people employed. Right?

From the lender's perspective, however, you represent a risk. Yes, your business is sought after, but the lender takes a chance by giving you something now for a promise to pay later. If you fail to keep your promise, the lender loses.

The degree of doubt between the lender making money and losing money dictates the terms of the credit. But how does a lender gauge the likelihood of your paying on time and as promised? The lender needs to know three pieces of information about you to gauge the risk you represent:

_____

_____

_____

- **Your character:** Do you do what you promise? Are you reliable and honest?
- **Your capacity:** How much debt can you handle, given your income and other obligations?
- **Your collateral:** What cash or property could you use to repay the debt if your income dries up?

But where can this information be had — especially if the lender doesn't know your sterling attributes firsthand? The answer: your credit report and, increasingly, your credit score. That's why, before you open that line of credit that allows you to buy the new dining room set on a 90-day-same-as-cash special, you have to fill out and sign some paperwork and wait a few minutes for your credit to be checked out.

Sometimes, however, an unscrupulous creditor may try to take advantage of you and charge you more than the market price for the credit you want. Why? Because they like to make money. So how do *you* know if you're being overcharged? The same way the lenders decide whether to offer you credit and what to charge you for it: by knowing what's in your credit report and your credit score.

_____

_____

_____

Credit's Cast of Characters

In most lending transactions, three players have lead roles: the buyer (that's you), the lender, and the credit reporter.

The buyer

The cycle of credit begins with the buyer — a person who wants something (that's you). A house, a car, a TV . . . it doesn't matter what you want; the definitive factor is that paying for it up front is either inconvenient or impossible. Maybe you just don't have the cash with you and you want the item now, or perhaps the item is on sale. Or maybe you haven't even earned the money to pay for the purchase, but you know you will and you don't want to pass up an opportunity.

"Hmm," you calculate as you gaze longingly at the coveted find. "I really want to get this now. If I wait until I have the money, it may be sold or the price may have gone up, so it only makes sense to buy it now."

Enter creditors, stage right.

The creditors

The creditor spots your desire a mile away, and it stirs the compassionate capitalist within him. "Hey," says the person with the power to extend you credit, "no need for you to do without. We have financing. We just need to take down a little information and do a quick credit check, and you can walk out the door with this thing you're lusting for."

If businesses can't sell you something or lend you money, they can't make a profit. So, believe it or not, they really do want to loan you money. But there's that risk factor: They need to find out how risky a proposition you may be. To get the low-down on your credit risk, they call the credit bureau.

Enter credit bureau, stage left.

The credit bureaus

The merchant most likely contacts one of three major credit-reporting bureaus — Equifax, Experian, or TransUnion (see Chapter 3 for more on these organizations) — to get the credit lowdown on you. The credit bureaus make the current lending system work by providing fast, reliable, and inexpensive information about you to lenders and others.

The information in your credit report is reported by lenders doing business with one or more bureaus and put into what is the equivalent of your electronic credit history file folder. This file of data is called your *credit report* (see Chapter 3).

Over the years, as more information has built up in credit reports and faster decision-making has been found to result in more sales, lenders have increasingly looked for shortcuts in the underwriting process that still offer protection from bad lending decisions. Thus emerged the *credit score*, a shorthand version of all the information in your credit report. The credit score predicts the likelihood of your defaulting on a loan. The lower the score, the more likely you are to default. The higher the score, the better the odds of an on-time payback. By far, the most-used score today is the FICO score. FICO scores range from 300 to 850.

The Consequences
of Bad Credit

Aside from the obvious increase in borrowing costs and maybe a hassle getting a credit card, what are the very real costs of bad credit? The extra interest you have to pay is only the tip of the iceberg. The real cost of bad credit is in having reduced opportunities, dealing with family stress, and having to associate with lenders who, more often than not, see you as a mark to be taken for a ride and dumped before you do it to them. And they're better at it than you are. This section fills you in on some of the unpleasant consequences of bad credit.

Paying fees

From your perspective as the borrower in trouble, extra fees make no sense. You're having a short-term problem making ends meet, so what do your creditors do to help you? They add some fat fees onto your balance.

How do these fees help you? They don't. The fees help the *creditor* in two ways:

- They focus your attention on *that creditor's* bill instead of someone else's.

- The creditor gets compensated for the extra risk you've just become.

As bad as the fees can be on your credit cards, they can be even worse on your secured loans. If you fall three months behind in your house payment, you can be hit with huge fees, to the tune of thousands of dollars.

Secured lenders tend to be low-key. Don't let that calm voice or polite, nonthreatening letter lull you into complacency. They're low-key because they don't *have* to shout — they'll very quietly take your home or other collateral, unlike the credit card guys, who can be heard from across the street. Pay attention to the quiet guy, and take action early.

Late fees, overlimit fees, legal fees, repo fees, penalty fees, deficiency payments, and default rates — when the fees show up, it's time to get serious. Call the creditor and ask to have the fees waived. Explain your plan to get current (make any past-due payments) and let them know that you need their help, not their fees Escalate your complaint to a supervisor, if needed. Chapter 4 helps you put together a budget so you know exactly how much you can afford. If you have difficulty developing a budget, your creditors may accept a debt-management plan, which you work out with the help of a credit-counseling agency. Take action early enough in the game, while you and your account are still considered valuable assets, and you're more likely to have success getting the fees removed.

Being charged higher interest rates

Consider two home buyers, one with a credit score of 760, the other with a credit score of 659. The happy new homeowner with the lower score won't be so happy to learn that, because of that lower score, he'll pay more than $90,000 more in interest over the life of the loan. Why? Because the mortgage company offers an interest rate of 5.3 percent to the individual with the 760 score, and an interest rate of 6.6 percent to the borrower with the 659 score.

The concept works basically the same in any lending situation. What impact would these scores have on a new car loan? A 36-month interest rate is more than *50 percent higher* for the person with the 659 score versus the one with the 760 score!

Your credit score is based on your credit actions yesterday, last year, and maybe even ten years ago. If you miss a payment or two, that low-interest-rate credit card on which you're carrying a high balance can take your breath away. Watch the rate climb to the mid- to upper-20s or even 30-something — *percent*, that is. Each state has a different maximum rate. Go to http://statelaws.findlaw.com/consumer-laws/ interest-rates.html for more information. After all, you made a mistake and may stop paying altogether. So the lender is going to make money on interest while it can.

You think that getting your interest rate hiked for a minor infraction is unfair? That's not the end of it. Under the policy of *universal default*, if you have an issue with one lender, all your other lenders can hike their rates as well — even though you're still paying the others on time and as agreed. In fact, some companies even use a deteriorated credit score as reason to escalate your rates to the penalty level. Even though you're paying that loan on time, a change in your credit score (perhaps from too many account inquiries or carrying higher balances) gives the creditor that has a universal default policy full rein to hike up your interest rates. This scenario is all the more reason to pay all bills on time and to keep track of your credit report and credit score on a regular basis.

Losing employment opportunities

Prospective lenders aren't the only ones who judge you based on your credit report and credit score. Potential employers check out your credit report, too. Why is that, you ask? Businesses reason that the way you handle your finances is a reflection of your behavior in other areas of your life. If you're late paying your bills, you may be late for work. If you default on your car loan, you may not follow through with an important assignment.

Even if your credit woes can be explained, bad credit is a distraction, from the employer's perspective, and it detracts from worker productivity. Research shows that employees with credit problems are significantly less productive on the job than employees without.

Increasingly, credit checks are a standard part of the hiring — and even promotion — process at companies large and small throughout the United States. And from the employer's perspective, it's easier to hire someone with good credit than to bother to find out what's going on with someone whose credit is bad.

Facing increased insurance premiums

The brain trusts at insurance companies (known as *actuaries*) love their numbers. They sniff out a trend and slap a charge on it faster than a cat can catch a mouse. The fact that a strong correlation exists between bad credit and reported claims hasn't escaped the attention of these people. The upshot: Bad credit will cost you a bundle in insurance-premium increases and may result in your being denied insurance.

Some states have gotten very excited about safe drivers and homeowners getting premium increases with no claims being reported. About 50 percent of states have restricted the use of credit-based insurance scores (and, to a lesser extent, credit reports) in setting insurance prices. To find out whether (and to what extent) scores and credit reports are used in your state, contact your local state insurance department.

This is not your garden-variety credit score here. Fair Isaac has developed an Insurance Score. This score is calculated by taking information from your credit report, but the formula differs from the one used to figure your typical credit score. Insurance scores range from 500 to 997, with 626 to 775 being average. The Federal Trade Commission weighed in on the topic when a study it conducted found that these scores are effective predictors of the claims that consumers will file.

Getting a divorce

Would your better half dump you because of bad credit? Maybe not, but one thing is sure: Half of all marriages end in divorce, and the biggest cause of fighting in marriages is due to financial issues — such as bad credit.

_____

_____

_____

Spouses want to be proud of their mates. And with credit playing a bigger role in so many aspects of modern American life, living with bad credit has to be a real blow to your image and self-esteem. Couples who are serious about pursuing a life together should talk about their attitudes on money and credit use. Sweeping this topic under the rug is too easy. Having a credit card refused for payment (often in front of others), worrying about which card still has available credit, or getting collection calls in the sanctuary of your home can be part of the credit nightmare you face as a couple. If you can't seem to find the words to talk about this sensitive topic or agree on a solution, get some professional advice before it becomes too late.

Consider this advice on bad credit and marriage:

- Get a credit report before you marry.
- Discuss money and credit, and agree on goals.
- Find out whether your partner is a spender or a saver.
- Fix your credit before it fixes you.

A Thin Credit File

Are you new to credit? Is your credit history file a tad thin? A *thin file* means that you don't have enough information in your credit file on which to base a credit score or make an underwriting decision. Typically, people who have just graduated from school, who are recently divorced or widowed, or who are new to the country have a thin file. The good news is that this group of newbies is so large and potentially profitable in today's comparatively saturated credit market that they've been given their own name — the *underbanked*. Basically, the underbanked are individuals who don't have access to the basics of the banking system, such as checking and savings accounts and credit services.

Don't confuse underbanked with *subprime*. The folks in the underbanked group don't have blemished credit histories. They simply don't have much, if any, credit history. A better term may be *preprime*. This section takes a closer look at some of the subgroups among the underbanked who have thin credit files and discusses some important points.

When you're new to the country

Individuals who are new to the United States may bring old attitudes about banks with them. Well, not only does the Statue of Liberty welcome you, but so do many banks and lenders. Furthermore, many immigrants have to overcome misconceptions and understand that, in the United States, banks are safe and insured for deposits, currency doesn't become worthless overnight, and the government is unlikely to nationalize the banks.

Social classes don't carry much weight in American banking. Anyone who walks into a bank or credit union gets treated with respect, regardless of what they do for a living. In fact, in many states with large-enough concentrations of immigrants, banking services are being offered in different languages and in informal community settings, not just traditional banking offices.

Credit is essential to making a full and comfortable life in the United States. Lending, employment, insurance, and more are tied into establishing a positive credit history. The American

Dream is intimately related to the credit system. So where do you start? Here are some points to consider:

- You don't need a Social Security number to open a bank account if you are a foreign national. A consular ID or taxpayer identification number is sufficient for many banks.
- Credit bureaus don't require a Social Security number to establish a credit history for you. Name, address, and date of birth all come before the Social Security number when it comes to linking credit histories with individuals.
- Credit doesn't consider race, national origin, gender, or any of those discriminatory categories.
- Building a relationship with a mainstream lender can help you avoid overpaying for credit products.

After one of life's many transitions

People who have just graduated or gone through a divorce also often have thin credit files. If you fall into this category, you're probably looking for ways to build your credit history. To begin your journey, set some long-term and interim goals as your destinations. Financial goals, like traveling goals, make sense, if only to keep you from wandering aimlessly. A car, a better apartment, a home, or a vacation are all good goals and reasons to save your money and use credit wisely.

 You can also do the following to help you begin to build credit:

- **Establish credit easily using a secured credit card.** You make a deposit into an insured bank account and are given a credit card with a limit up to the amount of your deposit. Your deposit guarantees payment and allows you to have positive credit reported in your name. Soon you'll qualify for an unsecured card and larger credit lines.

- **Open a passbook loan.** With a passbook loan, you make a deposit into a savings account and take out a small loan using the account as security. You don't use a credit card — you just get a lump-sum payment. But you can build a credit history when you make your payments on time, over time. Plus, the secured nature of the loan keeps costs very low. Credit unions, in particular, like these little starter loans.

_____

_____

_____

Identity Theft: The Crime That Turns Good Credit Bad

Companies and schools seem to be losing the war on hackers and laptop thieves who are reported to be compromising databases with alarming frequency. Identity theft can devastate your credit and your ability to get loans, employment, insurance, and some security clearances and licenses without your ever having done anything to deserve it. An identity theft can also put you on the defensive, burdening you with the responsibility of proving that you are not the person collectors are after.

Protect your identity from theft

 To avoid the havoc wreaked by identity theft, your best bet is to avoid being a victim of identity theft altogether. Consider these tips:

- **Protect your financial information at home.** Don't leave credit card numbers and statements, Social Security information, bank account information, and other financial data unprotected. Most identity theft is low-tech (that is, paper-based). And most is carried out by people you know: friends, relatives, acquaintances, co-workers, and people you invite into your home for a variety of reasons.

Shred statements before putting them in the trash and lock away your sensitive information. Using your computer more (as long as you use it properly, password-protect information, and use a firewall on your home network) is an even better way to avoid theft.

- **Watch the mail.** Most people think that no one is watching their unprotected mailboxes. And most are right, but that leaves the rest of you with sensitive account numbers and documents containing your Social Security number sitting all day in an unlocked mailbox outside your home or apartment. By comparison, electronic bill-paying is much safer. Sign up for alerts online for your bank accounts and credit cards where you get text or email messages for unusual activity. Use distinct passwords for sites where personal info is stored.

Take action if you're victimized

If you're a victim of identity theft, you may first discover that fact through a collection call on an account you never opened, or unusual activity on a credit card or credit report. When you suspect your identity has been compromised, respond immediately. Here are some tips:

- **Write down everything.** This process may not be quick or simple, but it is critical.
- **Call any creditors affected and close your accounts.** Don't forget ATM and debit cards — you have higher limits of liability for these cards than you do credit cards, so they're particularly important.
- **Freeze your credit report.** (You can unfreeze it later.) Each bureau has a slightly different process, but in general you request by certified mail that a security freeze be placed on your credit file. Your request should include your name, address, date of birth, Social Security number, proof of current address such as a current utility bill, and any payment of applicable fees. Details can be found at each bureau's website.
- **Call the police and make a report.** Some creditors and collectors require a report to take action. Be sure to get a copy of the report.

_____

_____

_____

3

Fixing Your Credit Report

Today, with tightening credit, a larger-than-usual need to refinance a home by a larger-than-usual percentage of the population, and credit card debt at very high levels, your credit report and score are at center stage. This chapter explains why you need to be on intimate terms with your credit report.

Why a Credit Report Is Important

Your credit report doesn't come into play just when you want to borrow money. A bad credit report may affect what you pay for insurance, whether you can rent the apartment of your choice, or whether you'll be hired for certain jobs. Clearly, what you don't know *can* hurt you.

You can't rewrite your credit history, but you *can* know what a credit report is and how much weight it carries as you try to negotiate your way through the financial universe. You *can* be savvy about situations that could cost you thousands of dollars more or deny you opportunities. And you *can* catch inaccuracies on your report and correct them.

Getting a current copy of your credit report from each of the three credit bureaus (Equifax, Experian, and TransUnion) is easy. And you can now request your credit report from each credit bureau once a year for *free*. So what's in your report? Is the information correct or even yours? If not, what can you do to fix it? Settle in for some facts that will save you money, time, and frustration.

What Is a Credit Report?

Your credit report is your financial life history of borrowing money. Credit-reporting bureaus gather, manage, maintain, and share this information. As many as 20 credit-reporting bureaus exist, but the following three are the biggies:

- **Equifax** (www.equifax.com; 800-685-1111)
- **Experian** (www.experian.com; 888-397-3742)
- **TransUnion** (www.transunion.com; 800-888-4213)

What your credit report says about you

As a snapshot of your financial life, your credit report may also indirectly predict your potential behaviors in other areas of your life. The fact that you have a history of making credit card payments late may tell a prospective landlord that you're likely to be late with your rent, too. If you've declared bankruptcy because your finances are out of control, perhaps you're out of control in other ways, too.

This snapshot, which brings into focus the details of your spending and borrowing and even suggests your personal life patterns, also paints a *bigger* picture of two important factors — characteristics critical to employers, lenders, and others.

Do you do what you promise?

Your credit history is an indicator of whether you're someone who follows through with commitments — a characteristic important to most people, whether they're looking for a reliable worker, a dependable renter, or a faithful mate. Needless to say, a person or company who is considering lending you a sizable sum of money will want to know the same.

Based largely on your history of following through with your financial promises, you're assigned a credit score. People with higher scores generally get the best terms, including lower interest rates and reduced minimum down payments. People with lower credit scores may not get credit in today's economy, unless they pay higher interest rates and possibly additional fees or insurance. Even then, they may not qualify for anything, under tight approval guidelines, particularly for mortgages.

Do you do it on time?

When it comes to your credit score, following through with your promises is only half of the game. The other half is doing it on time. In the lending business, the more overdue the payment is, the more likely it will not be paid at all — or paid in full. This fact is why, as you get further behind in your payments, lenders become more anxious about collecting the amount you owe. If you're sufficiently delinquent, the lender may want you to pay back the entire amount at once instead of as originally scheduled. (When it comes to money, your creditors' faith in you is only 30 to 90 days long. Car dealers see the end of the world happening in credit terms in a payment that's late by as little as two weeks.) So the longer you take to do what you promised, the more it costs you and the more damage you do to your credit score.

Uncover your credit report's details

The information in your credit report is specific, purely factual, and limited in scope. What it lacks in scope, however, it makes up for in sheer volume of material and the length of time it covers. If students cut a class, chances are no one will notice, but if they fail to pay a bill on time, a multibillion-dollar industry will notice, record it, and tell everyone who asks about them for the next seven years.

Consider the short take on what's in your credit report:

- **Personal identification information,** such as your name, Social Security number, date of birth, addresses (present and past), and most recent employment history. Be consistent with your information, especially how you spell your name and address. Name, address, and date of birth are the most common sources used to identify which file is yours. Social Security number is fourth.

- **Public-record information** on tax liens, judgments, bankruptcies, child-support orders, and other official info.

- **Collection activity** for accounts that have been sent to collection agencies for handling.

- **Information about each credit account,** open or closed (also known as *trade lines*), such as whom you owe, the type of account (such as a mortgage), whether the account is *joint* (shared with another person) or just in your name, how much you owe, your monthly payment, how you've paid (on time or late), and your credit limits.

- **A list of the companies that have requested your credit file for the purpose of granting you credit:** Requests are known as *inquiries* and are one of two types. *Soft inquiries* are made for promotional purposes (for instance, when a credit card issuer wants to send you a hot offer). These inquiries don't appear on the version of your credit report that lenders see. They are on the consumer's copy that you get. *Hard inquiries* are made in response to a request from you for more or new credit. These inquiries *do* appear on the lender's copy of your credit report.

- **An optional message from you,** up to 100 words in length, that explains any extenuating circumstances for any negative listings on your report.

- **An optional credit score:** Your credit score is not really part of your credit report; it's an add-on that you have to ask for and possibly pay for. Your score probably is different for each credit report because of data differences. (The importance of your credit score is covered later in this chapter.)

Credit reports are easy to read, although there's still room for improvement. Each of the three major credit-reporting agencies reports credit information in its own unique format. The credit-reporting agencies compete with each other for business, so they have to differentiate their products.

Among the list of items *not* included in your credit report are your lifestyle choices, religion, national origin, political affiliation, sexual preferences, friends, and relatives. Also, the three major credit-reporting agencies do not collect or transmit data on your medical history, checking or savings accounts, brokerage accounts, or similar financial records.

You can see sample credit reports from Equifax, Experian, and TransUnion online at the sites listed here:

- **Equifax:** www.equifax.com
- **Experian:** www.experian.com
- **TransUnion:** www.transunion.com

Who uses the info in your credit report?

Every day, businesses rely on the information in your credit report to help them decide whether to lend you money and at what price (otherwise known as the *interest rate* and *loan terms*). It is an important tool that serves different purposes:

- For a lender, your credit report is a tool to determine how likely and able you are to repay a loan, and it's an indicator of how much interest and what fees to charge you based on the risk profile you represent — if you qualify for a loan or refinance at all.
- For an insurance company, your credit report is a tool to predict how likely you are to have an accident or have your house burn down, although some states have banned using credit scores for auto insurance.

_____

_____

_____

- For an employer, your credit report is a tool to predict whether you'll be a reliable and trustworthy employee.

- For a landlord, your credit report is a tool to determine whether you're likely to pay the rent on time or at all.

- For you, your credit report is a tool to help you understand how you've handled your finances in the past and how you're likely to handle them in the future.

Many people can look at this information and make an increasing number of significant decisions that can affect your life, so double-checking this information is essential.

How Bad Stuff Gets in Your Credit Report

Whether you're new to the world of credit or you're an experienced borrower, you need to keep a few key concepts in mind as you look over your credit report. The following sections help you focus on what matters and let go of what doesn't.

Nobody's perfect

You aren't perfect. The same goes for your credit report — and lack of perfection isn't a big deal, as long as your credit report shows more smooth patches than bumps. No matter how early you mail off that bill payment, it can still arrive late or get lost, which means you can expect to find some negative information on your credit report from time to time. The good news is that you can still be eligible for plenty of loans at competitive rates and terms without having a flawless credit report.

But how many bad marks are okay? How long do they stay? And how will lenders who view your report interpret them? For example, say you're a well-heeled, easygoing gal and you loan your boyfriend $5,000 for a very worthy cause. He promises to pay you back monthly over two years. But after four months without a payment, two things likely will happen: He'll no longer be your sweetie, and you'll have mentally written off any chance of collecting the debt. Plus, if you're smart, you'll think twice before lending money to a friend again. You may even mention the negative experience to your friends, especially if they were thinking of floating him a loan.

If you were to run into your ex-boyfriend sometime down the road, you'd probably mention the $5,000 — after all, you want your money back, and he still owes you. Whether you'd ask him to join you for dinner is another matter and may depend on his showing you some good-faith gesture.

In business, as in love, trust and faithful performance are keys to success. A creditor can tell your future and current creditors any repayment information that is correct and accurate through your credit report, in the same way that you can warn your friends about your ex-boyfriend. That information or warning may be modified at any time, as long as the new information is correct and accurate.

Just how much does a mistake cost you when it comes to your credit report? Well, it depends on your history. Along with the credit report and all the information that it contains, lenders can buy a *credit score* based on the information in the report. That score comes from a mathematical equation that evaluates much of the information on your credit report at that particular credit bureau. By comparing this information to the patterns in zillions of past credit reports, the score tells the lender your level of future credit risk. (Check out the later section "Credit score components" for more info.)

So people with a lot of information in their credit files will find that a lot of good credit experiences lessen the effect of a single negative item. If you're a young person or a new immigrant with only a few trade lines and a few months of credit history (sometimes called a *thin file*), a negative event has a much larger effect in relation to the information available. Many young people think the world is stacked against them. In this case, it's true — but to be fair, it's also stacked against anyone with a limited credit history, regardless of your age or what country you come from.

Check for errors

Other people make mistakes, too — even banks and credit card payment processors. Considering that about billions of pieces of data are added to credit reports every month, it shouldn't be a big surprise that incorrect information may show up on your credit report. And there is the unrelated problem of errors caused as a result of identity theft. A number of conflicting studies have been done on what percentage of reports contain errors and, of those errors, how many were serious enough to affect either the terms under which credit was granted or whether credit was granted at all. So you may or may not have errors on your report. And they may or may not be serious. But unless you're feeling really lucky, you should find out what's in your report.

Still, credit-reporting agencies have a vested interest in the accuracy of the information they report. They sell it, and their profits are on the line if their information is consistently inaccurate. If credit-reporting agencies consistently provide error-riddled data, companies that grant credit won't be as eager to pay money to get or use a bureau's credit reports.

Getting a copy of your credit report gives you a chance to check for these errors and — better yet — get them corrected. You can have inaccurate information removed by one of two methods: contacting the credit bureau or the creditor.

Contact the credit bureau

If you notice incorrect information on your credit report, contact the credit bureau that reported the inaccurate information. Each of the three major bureaus allows you to dispute information in your credit report on its website, or you can call the bureau's toll-free number (see "What Is a Credit Report?" earlier in this chapter). If you make your dispute online, you need to have a copy of your credit report available; the report includes information that allows the bureau to confirm your identity without a signature. If you opt to call the toll-free number, you're unlikely to get a live person on the other end — this stuff is heavily automated — but you'll be told what information and documentation you need so that you can submit a written request. After you properly notify the credit bureau, you can count on action.

The Fair Credit Reporting Act (FCRA) requires credit-reporting agencies to investigate any disputed listings. The credit bureau must verify the item in question with the creditor *at no cost* to you, the consumer. The law requires that the creditor respond and verify the entry within 30 days, or the information must be removed from your credit report. The credit-reporting agency must notify you of the outcome. If information in the report has been changed or deleted, you also get a *free* copy of the revised report.

Contact the creditor

The Fair and Accurate Credit Transactions Act (commonly referred to as the FACT Act or FACTA) covers another way to remove inaccurate information from your credit report. Under the provisions of the FACT Act, you can deal directly with the creditor that reported the negative information in the first place. Contact information is shown on your latest billing statement from that creditor.

Do everything in writing, return-receipt requested. After you dispute the information, the reporting creditor must look into the matter and cannot continue to report the negative information while it's investigating your dispute.

For new delinquencies, the FACT Act requires that you be notified if negative information is reported to a credit bureau. That said, you may have to look closely to even see this new notice. Anyone who extends credit to you must send you a one-time notice either before or not later than 30 days after negative information — including late payments, missed payments, partial payments, or any other form of default — is furnished to a credit bureau. This stipulation also applies to collection agencies, as long as they report to a credit bureau. The notice may look something like this:

- **Before negative information is reported:** "We may report information about your account to credit bureaus. Late payments, missed payments, or other defaults on your account may be reflected in your credit report."

• **After negative information is reported:** "We have told a credit bureau about a late payment, missed payment, or other default on your account. This information may be reflected in your credit report."

The notice is not a substitute for your close monitoring of your credit reports, bank accounts, and credit card statements.

Look at the accurate information

Most of the information in your credit report likely is accurate. A popular misconception is that data stays on your credit report for seven years and then drops off. What really happens is that negative data stays on your credit report for seven years, although a few items remain longer, such as a Chapter 7 bankruptcy, which stays on your report for ten years. Even though the negative information is included for a long time, as the months and years roll by, it becomes less important to your credit profile. The fact that you were late in paying your credit card bill one time three years ago doesn't concern most creditors. Positive information, however — the good stuff everyone likes to see — stays on your report for a much longer time. Some positive data may be on your report for 10, 20, or even

30 years, depending on whether you keep your account open and depending on each bureau's policy.

Unscrupulous lenders may use negative information as a reason to put you into a higher-cost loan, even though you qualify for a less-expensive one. This is just one example of a situation in which understanding your credit score can save you money. The scenario can go something like this: You're looking for a loan for a big-ticket item. Instead of going from bank to bank and wasting days of precious free time or risking being turned down after filling out long applications and explaining about the $5,000 your ex-boyfriend owes you, you go to a trusted financial advisor who knows how these things work. She pulls your credit report and shops for a loan for you. She finds a loan, which she says is "a great deal considering your credit score." Translated, this statement means you're being charged a rate higher than the market rate because of your imperfect credit score. If you don't know what your score is and what rate that score entitles you to in the marketplace, you may be taken advantage of. So read on and get the skinny on credit scores, which have a big effect on your interest rates and terms.

_____

_____

_____

Your Credit Score

With billions of pieces of data floating around, it's little wonder that the people who use this data to make decisions turned to computers to help make sense of it all. Starting back in the 1950s, some companies, including one called Fair Isaac Corporation, began to model credit data in hopes of predicting payment behavior. (A *model* uses a series of formulas based on some basic assumptions to simulate and understand future behavior or to make predictions.) Until recently, the three major credit bureaus offered different scoring models that Fair Isaac, the developers of the *FICO score,* created for them. Each one called the score by a proprietary name. Now they also use an identical credit-scoring model called the VantageScore. Your credit score is a three-digit number that rules a good portion of your financial life, for better or worse.

You may have no credit score if you don't have enough of a credit history. Understanding what factors into your credit score is an important step in ensuring that yours is the best it can be. This section takes a closer look at the two main types of credit scores — FICO and VantageScore — and helps you understand what makes them up.

Credit score components

For a score to be calculated, you need to have at least one account open and reporting for a period of time. In this category, the Vantage people have the current edge. They require that you have only one account open for at least 3 months, and that account must have been updated in the last 12 months. FICO requires you to have an account open (and updated) for at least six months. Although having no credit history makes it difficult for you to get credit initially, you'll find it a lot easier to build credit for the first time than to repair a bad credit history.

The most widely used of these credit scores is the FICO score. The proprietary formula for FICO scores was once a well-guarded secret. Creditors were concerned that if you knew the formula, you may be tempted to manipulate the information to distort the outcome in your favor. Well, that may or may not be the case, but if creditors are looking for good behavior on your part, it only makes sense to tell you what constitutes good behavior. In 2001, Fair Isaac agreed, with a little help from some regulators, and disclosed the factors and weightings used to determine your credit score.

FICO scores range from 300 to 850. The higher the number, the better the credit rating. FICO takes into account more than 20 factors when building your score; the importance of each depends on the other factors, the volume of data, and the length of your history. Your FICO score consists of five components:

- **Paying on time (35 percent):** Payment history is considered the most significant factor when determining whether an individual is a good credit risk. This category includes the number and severity of any late payments, the amount past due, and whether the accounts were repaid as agreed. The more problems, the lower the score.

- **Amount and type of debt (30 percent):** The amount owed is the next-most-important factor in your credit score. This factor includes the total amount you owe, the amount you owe by account type (such as revolving, installment, or mortgage), the number of accounts on which you're carrying a balance, and the proportion of the credit lines used. For example, in the case of installment credit, *proportion of balance* refers to the amount remaining on the loan in relation to the original amount of the loan. For revolving debt, such as a credit card, this amount is what you currently owe in relation to your credit limit. You want a low balance amount owed in relation to your amount of credit available. Having credit cards with no balances ups your limits and your score.

- **The length of time you've been using credit (15 percent):** The number of years you've been using credit and the type of accounts you have also influence your score. Accounts that have been open for at least two years help to increase your score.

- **The variety of accounts (10 percent):** The mix of credit accounts is a part of each of the other factors. Riskier types of credit mean lower scores. For example, if most of your debt is in the form of revolving credit or finance-company loans, your score will be lower than if your debt is from student loans and mortgage loans. Also, the lender gives more weight to your performance on its type of loan. So a credit card issuer looks at your experience with other cards more closely, and a mort-gagee pays closer attention to how you pay mortgages or secured loans. An ideal mix of accounts has many types of credit used.

_____

_____

_____

- **The number and types of accounts you've opened recently, generally in the last six months or so (10 percent):** The number of new credit applications you've filled out, any increases in credit lines that you requested (unsolicited ones don't count), and the types and number of new credit accounts you have affect your credit score. The reasoning is that if you're applying for several accounts at the same time and you're approved for them, you may not be able to afford your new debt load.

One entrant to the scoring field is the VantageScore. Vantage needs 3 months of history and an update in the last 12 months for a score. VantageScore's range is from 501 to 990. Your VantageScore is made up of six components:

- **Payment history (32 percent):** Again, payment history is the most significant factor when determining whether an individual is a good credit risk. Your history includes satisfactory, delinquent, and derogatory items.

- **Utilization (23 percent):** This factor refers to the percentage of your available credit that you have used or that you owe on accounts. Using a large proportion of your overall available credit has a negative effect.

_____

_____

_____

- **Balances (15 percent):** This area includes the amount of recently reported current and delinquent balances. Balances that have increased recently can be an indication of risk and can lower your score.

- **Depth of credit (13 percent):** The length of history and types of credit used are included. A long history with mixed types of credit is best.

- **Recent credit (10 percent):** The number of recently opened credit accounts and all new inquiries are considered. New accounts initially lower your score; companies initially aren't sure why you want more credit. However, after you use the accounts and pay on time, they can help raise your score by adding positive info.

- **Available credit (7 percent):** This factor refers to the amount of available credit for all your accounts. Using a low percentage of the total amount of credit available to you is good.

If you're trying to build a credit history for the first time, you're an immigrant, or you're in the FBI's Witness Protection Program and you're looking for your first unsecured credit card in your new name, look for a lender that uses a VantageScore to grant credit after you have established a credit record. Examples of ways to start a credit history include using a secured card or using a passbook loan.

If you're too thin: The Expansion score

It used to be that if you didn't have much information in your credit file, known as a *thin file* in the business, you were in a pickle. Lenders had a more difficult time assessing your risk because they couldn't get a score for you.

The *Expansion score* is a credit-risk score based on nontraditional consumer credit data (in other words, it's not based on data from the three major national credit bureaus). The purpose of this new score is to predict the credit risk of consumers who don't have a traditional FICO score. The use of FICO Expansion scores gives millions of new consumers who don't have extensive credit histories an opportunity to access credit. This category includes the following people, roughly one of four U.S. adults:

- Young people just entering the credit market
- New arrivals and immigrants to the United States
- People who previously had mostly joint credit and are now widowed or divorced
- People who've used cash instead of credit most or all of the time

4

Building and Sticking to a Budget

A *budget* is nothing more than a written plan for how you intend to spend your money each month, how much you'll contribute to savings and retirement, and so on. A budget helps you live within your means. It doesn't have to be scary. When you're drowning in debt, a budget is your financial life raft.

This chapter shows you how to create a monthly household budget and monitor your compliance with it. If you can't afford to pay all your obligations in a certain month, you find out which debts to pay and which to put off. You're also warned against using certain types of loans to generate extra cash.

If you stick to your budget and follow the rest of the advice in this book, your financial situation will improve. But even when your financial outlook is rosier, you should continue to manage your money by using a budget. Otherwise, you may get careless about your spending or begin using credit too much, and your debt may creep back up to dangerous levels.

Monthly Spending and Income

Creating a monthly budget for your household is not a complicated process, but it can be time consuming. Simply stated, you need to do this:

- Compare your current total monthly spending to your current total monthly income.
- Reduce your spending as necessary so that it's less than your income.
- Allocate your dollars appropriately so that you are able to pay all your living expenses and debts.

In Chapter 1, you're asked to compare your annual spending to annual income to start getting a fix on the state of your finances. If you haven't already completed this exercise, do so now; that information is essential to the budgeting process in this chapter. Then follow these steps:

1. **Divide each of the annual dollar amounts in Table 1-1 by 12 to come up with monthly amounts.**

2. **Make photocopies of the spending and income worksheet in Table 4-1 so you can use it multiple times.**

3. **Record each monthly amount in the appropriate worksheet space.**

4. **Review the dollar amounts, and adjust them up or down as necessary so they're as accurate as possible.**

   For example, the cost of your auto insurance may be about to increase, your child's tuition may be increasing next month, or your income may be decreasing. Always assume the worst scenario so that you build in a potential cushion.

   If your annual totals don't include living expenses and debts that you should be paying but aren't because you don't have enough money, add them to your annual totals before you divide by 12. For budget-building purposes, you *must* have an accurate picture of *all* your living expenses and debts.

5. **Subtract your total monthly spending from your total monthly income.**

   Record that amount on the worksheet; it can be a negative number.

Monthly Income	
Your household take-home pay	$_____
Child support income	$_____
Alimony income	$_____
Other income (specify the source)	$_____
Other income (specify the source)	$_____
Other income (specify the source)	$_____
Total Monthly Income	$_____
Monthly Spending	
Fixed Spending	
Rent	$_____
Mortgage	$_____
Home equity loan	$_____
Condo or homeowner's association fee	$_____
Car payment	$_____
Other loans	$_____

Table 4-1: *Monthly Spending and Income Worksheet*

Fixed Spending	
Homeowner's insurance	$_____
Renter's insurance	$_____
Health insurance	$_____
Auto insurance	$_____
Life insurance	$_____
Other insurance	$_____
Childcare	$_____
Dues and fees	$_____
Cable/satellite service	$_____
Internet access	$_____
Child support obligation	$_____
Alimony obligation	$_____
Other fixed expenses (specify type)	$_____
Other fixed expenses (specify type)	$_____
Other fixed expenses (specify type)	$_____
Other fixed expenses (specify type)	$_____
Total Monthly Fixed Spending	$_____
Variable Spending	
Groceries	$_____
Cigarettes	$_____
Alcohol	$_____
Utilities	$_____
Cellphone	$_____
Gas for car	$_____

(continued)

Variable Spending	
Public transportation	$_____
Tolls and parking	$_____
Newspapers, books, and magazines	$_____
Allowances	$_____
After-school activities for kids	$_____
Babysitting	$_____
Entertainment	$_____
Restaurant meals	$_____
Personal care products	$_____
Clothing	$_____
Body care (haircuts, manicures, massages)	$_____
Laundry and dry cleaning	$_____
Out-of-pocket medical expenses	$_____
Lawn care	$_____
Home repair and maintenance	$_____
Other (specify type)	$_____
Other (specify type)	$_____
Other (specify type)	$_____
Other (specify type)	$_____
Total Monthly Variable Spending	$_____
Periodic Spending	
Insurance	$_____
Auto registration and inspection	$_____
Subscriptions	$_____

Table 4-1 *(continued)*

Periodic Spending	
Charitable donations	$_____
Tuition	$_____
Dues and fees	$_____
Income taxes	$_____
Property taxes	$_____
Other (specify type)	$_____
Other (specify type)	$_____
Other (specify type)	$_____
Other (specify type)	$_____
Total Monthly Periodic Spending	$_____
Monthly Contributions	
Savings	$_____
Retirement	$_____
Other (specify type)	$_____
Other (specify type)	$_____
Other (specify type)	$_____
Other (specify type)	$_____
Total Contributions	$_____
Total Monthly Spending and Contributions	$_____
Total Monthly Income	$_____
minus	–
Total Monthly Spending and Contributions	$_____
equals	=
Your Bottom Line	$_____

A Budget Deficit

If the "Your Bottom Line" number in Table 4-1 is negative, you have a *budget deficit.* You may be making up the difference between your monthly income and your monthly spending by using credit cards, paying bills late, and so on. Stop those things; they're only driving you deeper into debt.

Cut expenses

Deal with your budget shortfall instead by reducing your spending. Review your budget, looking for expenses you can trim or eliminate. Focus first on your discretionary spending because those are nonessential items. You'll find most of your discretionary spending items in the "Variable Spending" category on your worksheet; however, some of your fixed and periodic spending items may also be discretionary. For example, cable TV is not an essential expense. Likewise, you may be able to find a cheaper Internet provider (or go to the library when you need the Internet) and cancel some of your memberships.

If your deficit is small and most of it is due to waste and fluff, you may be able to move your budget into the black just by eliminating nonessentials — but maybe not. Instead, you may have to go through several rounds of budget-cutting and do some serious belt-tightening before your household's total monthly spending is less than its total monthly income. Use your worksheet to calculate the impact of each round of cuts on your budget's bottom line.

For more spending-reduction suggestions, check out the ideas in Chapter 5.

Reduce debt before saving

If you contribute to a savings and/or a retirement plan, stop doing that for now. Use that money to cover your living expenses and pay down your high-interest debts. Why? The money in your savings and retirement accounts earns only a small amount of interest each month — most likely far less than the interest rates on your debts. When you have debt, every month you pay more in interest than you can earn in interest on your savings, and you fall further behind.

When your financial situation improves, start contributing to savings and retirement again as soon as possible.

But for now, you must put every penny you have toward your essential living expenses and toward paying down your high-interest debts.

Other strategies

Moving your budget from red to black may require more than budget-cutting alone. The same is true if you can afford to pay only the minimum due on your high-interest debts. When you pay just the minimum each month, it takes months, if not years, to pay off those debts, and you pay hundreds or even thousands of dollars in interest — dollars that you could put to better use. What else can you do? You can try the following:

- **Increasing your household income:** Get a second job, turn your hobby into a part-time business, participate in the gig environment (driving for Lyft or doing freelance work on Fiverr), sell nonessential possessions to raise cash, or let your boss know that you would like to work more hours. If your spouse or partner is not working outside the home, discuss whether a paying job makes sense — at least, until your finances improve.

- **Negotiating with your creditors:** Some of them may be willing to lower your monthly payments or make other changes to help you afford to continue paying on your debts.

- **Consolidating your debts:** Debt consolidation involves borrowing money to pay off high-interest debt and lower the total amount you pay on your debts each month.

- **Getting help from a reputable nonprofit credit-counseling agency:** Such agencies can help you develop your budget and may also suggest that you set up a debt-management plan.

- **Filing for bankruptcy:** Bankruptcy should always be your option of last resort. It may become your best option if you're about to lose an important asset or if your monthly expenses are so much higher than your income that it will take years of sacrifice and bare-bones budgeting before your debts are manageable and you have a little extra money left over each month.

After reviewing your financial information, a bankruptcy attorney can tell you whether you should file for bankruptcy and which type of bankruptcy you can file: a Chapter 13 reorganization, which gives you three to five years to pay your debts, or a Chapter 7 liquidation, which wipes out most of your debts. (To be eligible to file a Chapter 7, you must pass a federally required means test that takes into account your income and your expenses.)

If you decide to file bankruptcy, the attorney will inform you that within six months of doing so, you must go to a court-approved credit-counseling agency. The agency will make sure you understand your alternatives to bankruptcy and that there is no way that you can avoid having to file. If the agency concludes that bankruptcy is your only option, it will give you a certificate to provide to the bankruptcy attorney. The certificate permits you to file for bankruptcy. Without it you cannot pursue bankruptcy.

Pay the Important Stuff If You Can't Pay Everything

If you've cut your budget to the bare bones and you still can't afford to pay all your debts and cover all your living expenses, you have to decide what you will and won't pay. Here's how to prioritize:

_____

_____

_____

- **Essential living expenses:** Your essential living expenses belong at the top of your "Bills to Pay" list, including putting bread on your table, keeping a roof over your head, keeping your utilities on, and gassing up your car if you need it to earn a living. However, make sure that you have reduced those expenses as much as you possibly can.

- **Secured debts:** Your secured debts also belong at the top of the list of things to pay. Keep reading if you aren't sure what a secured debt is.

- **Certain unsecured debts:** Some of your unsecured debts should take priority over others. The later section "When to prioritize an unsecured debt" goes into more detail.

Secured versus unsecured debt

A *secured* debt is a debt that you collateralized with an asset that you own. (The asset is often referred to as your *collateral.*) When you collateralize a debt, the lender puts a lien on that asset, which gives the lender the legal right to take the asset if you fall behind on your payments. For example, if you have a mortgage loan, your lender has a lien on your home. If you have a car loan, the lender has a lien on your vehicle.

_____

_____

_____

A lot of your debt, like credit card debt, is probably *unsecured*, which means that the creditors do not have liens on any of your assets. If you don't pay an unsecured debt, the creditor will try to get you to pay up. If you don't, the creditor may bring a debt collector on board to try to get your money. If you still don't pay, the creditor must sue you to get the court's permission to try to collect what you owe. The creditor can ask the court for permission to

- Seize one of your assets.
- Put a lien on an asset so you can't borrow against it or sell it without paying your debt.
- *Garnish* your wages (take a portion of them each pay period), assuming that wage garnishment is legal in your state.

When to prioritize an unsecured debt

Depending on your circumstances, you'll want to treat certain unsecured debts as top priorities, given the potential consequences of not paying them. These unsecured debts deserve priority treatment:

- **Child support, especially if it's court ordered.**

- **Federal income taxes.** Uncle Sam has almost unlimited powers to collect past-due tax debts.

- **State income taxes.** If you don't pay these taxes, your state can sue you, garnish your wages, or seize your property.

- **Property taxes and homeowner's insurance, if these expenses aren't included in your mortgage payments.** When you don't pay your property taxes, the taxing authority will eventually take your home. If your homeowner's insurance gets canceled for nonpayment, your lender will buy insurance for you, but the insurance will be very expensive, so the total amount of your monthly mortgage payments will increase.

- **Federal student loans.** The IRS can collect what you owe when you fall behind on your federally guaranteed student loans.

- **Your health insurance, if you're responsible for the payments.** Keeping up with your health insurance is especially important if you or a family member has an ongoing health problem. Without insurance, an expensive illness or accident could push you into bankruptcy.

- **Medical bills.** A growing number of healthcare providers, including hospitals, are getting very aggressive about collecting on their patients' past-due accounts. If you owe money to a healthcare provider, contact the provider to try to work out a plan for paying what you owe.

If one of your unsecured creditors turns over your debt to a debt collector, no matter how much the debt collector may hound and threaten you, do not give in to the collector's demands if paying the unsecured debt means you won't be able to pay your priority debts or living expenses.

A Budget Surplus

If your monthly spending and income comparison shows that you have money left over each month, don't break out the champagne just yet. You may have a surplus because you're not paying some of your bills or you're meeting some of your obligations by using credit cards. If this is the case, you must still reduce your spending so your income covers all your bills and living expenses each month.

A key aspect of getting out of debt is not using your credit cards. Sometimes you may have to use a card to pay for a financial emergency if you have no extra money in your budget and you have nothing in savings. But you should resolve to pay off the amount you charge as quickly as possible — the next month, if possible. And you should try not to charge anything more until you've wiped out the new credit card debt.

You may also have a surplus because you're paying only the minimum due on your outstanding credit card balances each month. You'll never get out of debt that way. If you have any surplus in your budget, use it to accelerate the rate at which you pay off the balances, starting with the highest-rate card.

Even if you can cover your monthly obligations without using credit cards and while paying more than the minimum due on your card balances, don't assume you shouldn't reduce your spending. You must be concerned about how much you owe to your creditors, or you probably wouldn't be reading this book. Cut back where you can, and use that additional money to pay off your debts as fast as you can, starting with the debt that has the highest interest rate. After you've paid off that one, focus on paying off the debt with the next-highest rate of interest, and so on. When you've paid down your high-interest debts, use your surplus to start building up your savings.

Finalize and Stick to Your Budget

When you've reduced your spending as much as you can and decided what you will and won't pay if you can't afford to pay everything, you can finalize your household budget. Make a fresh copy of the worksheet from Table 4-1. Label it "Monthly Household Budget" and record your revised monthly spending amounts, as well as your monthly income amounts. Now you have a written plan for what you're going to do with your money each month.

 Review the budget with your family members, and post it in a visible location so everyone can see it — maybe on a bulletin board in the family room or on the refrigerator.

Steel your resolve

Now comes the hard part: living according to your budget. Sticking to your budget won't be easy, but keep your eye on the prizes: less financial stress, fewer debts, less damage to your credit history, and (eventually) more money to spend the way you want.

As you go through each month, be mindful of every dollar you spend, every check you write, and every time you use your debit card or go to an ATM. Cut up your credit cards, or use them only in emergencies. Refer to your budget regularly to make sure you're staying on track. If you find that you have overspent in one area, try to compensate by reducing in another area.

If your kids ask for things you haven't budgeted for, remind them why your family is trying to spend less. If they're older, maybe they can earn money for what they want.

Carry a small notebook or some other small record-keeping device with you for writing down everything you purchase with cash, a debit card, or a credit card each day. Keep all your receipts as well. You'll need this information at the end of each month when it's time to evaluate how well you're doing.

_____

_____

_____

Check your progress each month

To live on a budget, each month you must compare your actual monthly spending to what you budgeted. Here's how:

1. **On your monthly budget, add a column to the right of each dollar amount that's labeled "Actual."**

2. **Compile all your spending records for the month (check registers, bank statements, receipts, and the information in your spending notebook) and all your income records to figure out your actual expense and income numbers.**

3. **Record these amounts in the appropriate places in the "Actual" column of your budget for the month.**

4. **Calculate subtotals and grand totals for the month.**

If you spent more than you budgeted on something, or if your total spending exceeded what you budgeted, try to figure out why you spent more. Here are some possible explanations:

- **You overlooked a living expense or debt when you developed your budget.**
- **Your budget isn't realistic.** It's too bare bones.

_____

_____

_____

- **Your family didn't try hard enough to live according to your budget.** Making a budget work takes a 100 percent commitment from everyone in your household.

- **You were hit with an unexpected expense that month.** For example, you were working late at the office, so your childcare expenses increased, or your car broke down and you had to spend money to fix it.

- **Some of your expenses increased for reasons beyond your control.** The cost of gas went up or your insurance premium increased, for example.

- **Your income dropped.** Maybe you had to take a cut in pay, your sales commissions were lower than usual, or a client didn't pay you.

Depending on your conclusions, you may need to revise some of the numbers in your household budget. If you have to increase the amount of an expense, try to decrease another expense by the same amount. If you have to revise your budget to reflect a decrease in your household's monthly income, try to offset the decrease with budget cuts as well.

If your monthly comparison shows that some of your expenses were lower than what you budgeted, don't revise

_____

_____

_____

your budget right away. Wait a month or two to see if the changes are permanent. If they are, put the extra money toward your high-interest debts, focusing first on paying off the debt with the highest rate of interest. Do the same if your income increases permanently.

Your budget is a dynamic document that should change as your finances change, hopefully for the better. Gradually, if you stick to your budget, you'll start paying off your debts faster. Eventually, you'll also be able to add some extras to your budget (maybe some of the things you've had to give up for now) and start contributing to savings so you'll have a financial safety net. If you continue to be careful about your spending and minimize your use of credit, your family will be in a position to make its financial dreams come true.

_____

_____

_____

5

Cutting Spending and Boosting Income

When your monthly expenses are greater than your income, you must rein in your spending and stop using your credit cards. The same is true if you're just barely getting by each month, if you're paying only the minimum due on your credit cards, or if you have little or nothing in savings. Finding ways to increase your income may also be essential. This chapter gives you practical suggestions for reducing your spending *and* boosting your income.

Find Ways to Spend Less

This section offers a treasure trove of ideas for spending less, organized by category of everyday expense: housing, utilities, food, transportation, healthcare, and so on. Some of the ideas are small and simple but yield big benefits over time, especially when done in combination with other money-saving suggestions.

Don't reject any cost-cutting ideas right off the bat, even if they mean major changes in your lifestyle and a lot of sacrifice. After you give up a few "essentials," you may discover that you don't even miss them.

Look for good deals

Although you should always try to buy things when they're on sale, you shouldn't buy an item just because it's discounted. Instead, make purchases based on whether you truly need an item. If you scan ads looking for good deals, you're bound to be tempted to buy things you don't really need. Keep this in mind: That item that looks like such a good deal today may get marked down even more in a week or two.

If you can't resist a sale, you may have a spending problem. People with spending problems tend to buy for the sake of buying, even when they know they shouldn't. Spending makes them feel good at the time but lousy later. Even so, they spend again. If you think you may have a spending problem, don't be embarrassed. Get help from other overspenders by going to a Debtors Anonymous (DA) meeting in your area. To find a chapter in your area, go to www.debtorsanonymous.org or call 781-453-2743.

Spend less on your housing

Housing is probably the single biggest item in your budget, especially if you are a homeowner and take into account the cost of maintenance, repairs, insurance, and taxes. You can rein in your housing costs in many ways.

Renters

Following are some options to consider if you're renting:

- If you're close to the end of your lease, find a cheaper place to live. If you've got time left on your lease, read your lease agreement to find out how much it costs to break it so you can move out early.

- Move in with relatives or friends while you improve your finances.

- Stay where you are but get a roommate, if allowed.

Homeowners

If you own your home, consider the following possibilities:

- Look into mortgage refinancing to lower your monthly payments. Be careful, however, about refinancing with a mortgage that may create problems for you down the road. If you're confused about whether a particular mortgage is good or bad for your finances, talk to a financial advisor, a nonprofit credit-counseling agency, or a real estate attorney.

- Rent out an extra room in your home.

- Lease your home to someone else and move into cheaper digs. Make sure the rent you charge covers your mortgage payments plus the cost of your homeowner's insurance, property taxes, and routine maintenance and repairs.

- Sell your home. This may be a lot to ask, but if you're paying for more house than you can truly afford, getting out from under the debt is a good thing.

Lower your utility bills

The cost of heating and cooling a home always seems to go up. Add the cost of water, wastewater, and lights, and you may find yourself gasping when you open your utility bills. Consider these suggestions for bringing down these costs:

- Use your heat and air conditioning less by keeping your home cooler in the winter and warmer in the summer.

- Lower the temperature on your water heater, but not to less than 120 degrees.

- Ask whether your local utility company offers free energy audits. You can find out where your house is losing energy and what you can do to make your home more energy efficient.

- Find out whether your utility offers an energy-saving program.

- Replace your commode with one that uses less water. Also replace old showerheads with new low-flow heads.

- Make your home more energy efficient by caulking, using weather stripping, and adding insulation, all of which are relatively easy do-it-yourself projects.

- Use fans, not air conditioning, to cool your home.

- Hang up your clothes to dry. Not only is using a dryer expensive, but all that hot air makes your clothes wear out faster.

- If you have to replace your washing machine, get one that loads from the front instead of the top. You'll reduce your energy use by as much as 50 percent and save on water.

- Take showers, not baths, and limit the length of your showers.

- Replace old-fashioned light bulbs with ultra-efficient fluorescent bulbs.

- Never run a dishwasher that is only half full.

- Fix leaky faucets.

Eat for less

One of the easiest expenses to reduce is the amount you spend on food. Reducing your grocery bill may mean eating more homemade foods and fewer prepackaged items, which has some added bonuses: You'll be eating healthier, and you'll probably shed a pound or two. Here are some tips:

_____

_____

_____

- Plan your meals for the coming week based on your budget, and go to the grocery store with a list of the items you need. Buy them and nothing more.

- Minimize your trips to the grocery store. The more trips you make, the more you're apt to spend.

- Never shop when you're hungry. You're more apt to load your cart with items you really don't need.

- When you make a meal, double the recipe and store the extra half in your freezer. When you have to work late one night, you'll be less tempted to purchase prepared food or carryout on your way home because you have a meal waiting that you can just pop into the microwave.

- Clip coupons for good deals on items you plan to buy. Coupon Web sites like www.couponcabin.com and www.couponcraze.com offer savings at specific stores and on popular national brands.

- Shop at several different grocery stores. Some may offer better deals on certain items that you use.

- Purchase house brands.

- Minimize your use of prepared foods and convenience items. You pay a premium for them.

_____

_____

_____

- If you drink alcohol regularly, drink less and buy less-expensive wine, beer, or hard liquor.

- Purchase groceries at warehouse stores, discount houses, and buying clubs. When practical, buy in bulk. But don't buy perishable items in large quantities unless you're sure you'll use them before they spoil. Also, don't buy items in bulk that you're not sure your family will use.

- Pack lunches for yourself and your family.

- Make your own morning coffee instead of buying it.

- Eliminate sodas and junk food from your diet.

- Reserve dining out for weekends or special occasions.

- Celebrate a special occasion with a picnic instead of a restaurant meal.

- Pop your own popcorn for the movies. Old-fashioned homemade popcorn tastes better than the stuff available at most movie theaters, and it's a lot cheaper, too.

- When your family goes on a day trip, pack your meal instead of eating at a restaurant.

- Grow your own vegetables and herbs. If you don't have a green thumb or if you lack the space for a garden, buy your fruits and veggies at your local farmers' market.

Pay less for transportation

After the cost of housing, the cost of getting from place to place may be your second-biggest monthly expense. You may already have found ways to trim your transportation budget, but you could well find some new ideas here:

- Use public transportation, ride your bike, walk, or carpool to work, if possible. If you use public transportation or carpool, you may be able to read and enjoy the scenery. If you ride your bike or walk, you may lose a few pounds.

- Shop around for the best deal on gas. Driving a little farther to fill your tank for less may be worth the extra miles and time. The free GasBuddy phone app can help you find the best price near you.

- If your vehicle is a gas guzzler or expensive to maintain, consider selling it and buying a less-expensive used vehicle.

- Change your own oil, and do your own simple car repairs. Your local community college or an adult education program in your area may offer a class in basic car maintenance, or maybe a friend can show you the basics.

_____

_____

_____

- Pump your own gas and wash your own car. Also, don't buy a higher grade of gas than your car really needs.

- Find a reliable mechanic who won't charge you an arm and a leg every time you bring your vehicle to the repair shop. Ask people you know, especially people who drive cars similar to yours, for the names of good mechanics. Avoid having your car repaired by a dealer or at a chain car repair shop.

- Ask your teenagers to pay for their own gasoline and auto insurance or to help contribute to the cost.

Have fun for less

Reducing your budget doesn't mean that you and your family have to eliminate fun from your lives. It means cutting out the frills and taking time to find affordable ways to have a good time. Consider these suggestions:

- Use your public library instead of buying books and DVDs, or swap these items with your friends.

- Commune with nature. Go for a hike, ride your bike, have a picnic in the park, go fishing, enjoy the babble of a swift running creek, and take time to enjoy the sunset.

_____

_____

_____

- Put together jigsaw puzzles, play card and board games, do crossword puzzles, play charades, create a scrapbook, or put all your photos into albums.
- Use your community pool.
- Take advantage of free events in your community.
- Entertain with potluck meals.
- Invite friends over for a backyard barbecue, and have everyone bring something to throw on the grill.
- Curl up with a good book.
- Use two-for-one coupons or share an entrée with your dinner companion when you want to dine out.
- Trade babysitting services with friends or relatives who also have young children to make going out occasionally more affordable.

Look good for less

When you're rolling in dough, you can afford to spend a bundle on salons, spas, personal trainers, and so on. But those are all luxuries you can't afford now. Here are suggestions for keeping yourself and your family looking good for less:

- Do your own manicures and pedicures, or get together with a girlfriend and do them for each other.

- Cut and color your own hair, get it cut and colored less frequently, or look on the web for a beauty school in your area. Most beauty schools offer free or low-cost cuts and coloring so students can hone their skills while being supervised by professionals.

- Get a massage at a massage school in your area.

- Eliminate expensive cosmetics, creams, and lotions. Drugstore items usually do the job.

- Minimize your use of dry cleaning, and wash and iron your own shirts, blouses, and pants. If you hate ironing, watch TV or listen to music while you work.

- If you belong to a health club and your membership is about to expire, find a less-expensive alternative or — if you rarely go — cancel your membership. Your local YMCA or community center may be an option.

- Give up your nightly wine or beer. They cost money, and they increase the number of calories you consume and jeopardize your health if you're a problem drinker.

Dress for less

With a little planning and ingenuity, you and the rest of your family members can look like fashion plates without paying top dollar. The key is to plan ahead, eliminate impulse buying, and maybe rethink where you shop. Consider these suggestions for how to look like a million dollars on the cheap:

- Shop only when you truly need clothes, not for fun or out of boredom.

- At the end of each season, take inventory of the clothing items you need to replace because they're worn out or because your kids have outgrown them. Then take advantage of end-of-season sales.

- Check out thrift shops, nearly-new stores, and yard sales.

- Buy on sale when possible, and shop at discount stores.

- If you have young children, make their clothes last longer by buying them a little big. Then roll up the sleeves and pants bottoms, and shorten the hems on skirts and dresses.

- Swap clothes with friends or family members.

Reduce your phone costs

Over the past decade or so, the amount of money you spend to stay in touch has probably increased. Cellphones are ubiquitous, and phone companies offer a plethora of extras that are nice but unnecessary. Therefore, reducing the amount you spend on your phone service each month may not be much of a challenge, and those reductions should have little or no real impact on your lifestyle. You can implement some of these suggestions for staying in touch for less:

- Shop around for the best deal on phone service. Websites like www.myrateplan.com can help you home in on your best options.

- Cancel your landline and go with Internet-based phone service through your cable company or a company like Vonage or Skype. Typically, you pay a flat fee for unlimited domestic calls. However, most of these companies require that you have high-speed Internet access, and you may need to purchase a headset; before you ditch your landline, put pencil to paper to be sure you'll save money.

• Make sure your calling plan matches the way you use your phone. For example, if you make a lot of in-state calls, your calling plan should have a low intrastate rate; if you frequently call out of state, be sure your plan offers low interstate rates. Some plans allow unlimited long-distance calling on weekends, in the evenings, or 24/7.

• Consider a family plan for your cellphone service if multiple people in your household have cellphones. Also ask your teens to pay for the cost of having a cellphone.

• Get rid of your landline if you have a cellphone with an unlimited calling plan.

• Review the extras you're paying for, like voicemail, call waiting, caller ID, and so on. Do you *really* need them?

• Minimize or eliminate your use of directory assistance.

Save on prescription drugs

If the cost of prescription drugs is taking a big bite out of your budget, don't do without — follow this advice for reducing what you pay for your pills:

- Ask your doctor for free samples whenever she prescribes a prescription drug for you or someone in your family.

- Ask your doctor whether a generic or less-expensive alternative to a drug is available.

- Buy 90-day supplies of drugs when you order to save on the dispensing fee that many pharmacies charge each time they fill a prescription.

- Talk with your doctor about prescribing a higher dose of the pill you normally take, and use a pill splitter to split it in half. You pay for fewer refills this way. However, your doctor should have the final say on whether this is a good option for your particular medication.

- Shop around before you get a prescription filled. You may be surprised by the range in prices from drugstore to drugstore.

- Purchase prescription drugs from an online pharmacy — one licensed by the National Association of Boards of Pharmacy through its VIPPS program. (The VIPPS seal of approval will be prominently displayed on the site.) Go to `https://nabp.pharmacy/` for a list of the online pharmacies it has licensed. Reputable online pharmacies include `www.costco.com` and `www.familymeds.com/online-pharmacy`.

- If you take medications regularly, buy in bulk from a mail-order pharmacy.

- Find out whether you qualify for a drug-assistance program. Some programs are income based, but others offer prescription drug discounts to consumers who are uninsured, regardless of their incomes. Partnership for Prescription Assistance at `www.pparx.org` offers an online databank of drug-assistance programs.

Drug discount cards tend to be bad deals, in part because they have so many restrictions. For example, you may not be able to use your card to buy generic drugs or buy drugs online, or you may be able to use it only at certain pharmacies.

Inch down your insurance costs

Maintaining your insurance coverage is essential even when you need to cut back. Without it, a serious illness, a car accident, or flood or wind damage to your home could be financially devastating and push you into bankruptcy.

Shop around for the best deal on your insurance. An insurance broker can help, or you can explore your options by using a website like www.insure.com. For example, you may be able to get less-expensive coverage by switching to another provider, by raising your *deductibles* (the amount of money you have to pay out of pocket before your insurance company starts to pay) on your current policies, or by getting rid of any insurance bells and whistles you don't need.

Also make sure you're getting all the insurance discounts you're entitled to. For example, you may be entitled to a discount if you don't commute to work in your car, if you purchase your home and auto insurance from the same company, if you're over 65, and so on.

Homeowner's insurance

Here are specific tips for reducing home insurance costs:

- When you insure your home, don't count the value of the land your home sits on. Insure the structure only.

- Find out whether you'll save money by installing deadbolt locks and smoke detectors. If your home has a security system, make sure it's reflected in your policy.

- If someone in your family was a smoker but has kicked the habit, find out whether your insurance company will lower your premium costs. Households with smokers often pay a premium for insurance because burning cigarettes are a leading cause of house fires.

Auto insurance

Consider these ways to trim your auto insurance bill:

- If your vehicle is old and not worth very much, drop your collision coverage, especially if you're spending more on the coverage than your car is worth. Another option is to increase the deductible amounts for your collision and comprehensive coverage.

- Be sure that you're getting all the discounts you may be entitled to, such as discounts for a car with antilock brakes, automatic seat belts, and airbags; a particular profession (statistics show that people in certain types of professions — engineers and teachers, for example — tend to have fewer accidents); or military service (some insurance companies give you a break on the cost of your insurance if you're in the military or used to be).

- If you have to purchase a new car, buy one like your grandmother might drive. High-profile/high-performance cars cost more to insure.

- Find out whether your association membership entitles you to a discount on your auto insurance.

Health insurance

Health insurance costs continue to skyrocket, and finding ways to reduce them can seriously help your household budget. Here are some suggestions:

- Talk with your employer's health plan administrator, or with your insurance broker or agent if you're not part of a group plan, about what you can do to lower your monthly health insurance costs. Possibilities may include increasing your annual deductible, switching insurance companies, or changing plans.

If you're willing to sacrifice the freedom to go to whatever doctor, pharmacy, or hospital you want, you can save money. Sign up with a plan that limits your choices; the more flexible, the more costly.

If someone in your family has a preexisting medical condition, don't change plans or insurers before you know how coverage for that condition may be affected. Some plans or providers may refuse to cover the condition at all or may not cover it for a period of time — six months to a year, for example.

Be aware that the insurance plan with the lowest premium cost is not a good deal if it doesn't offer the coverage and benefits you need. In the end, paying a little extra to have the appropriate coverage may mean lower out-of-pocket expenses for doctors, hospitals, and prescription drugs.

- If your income is low and you have few, if any, assets of value, find out whether you qualify for Medicaid, the federal/state health insurance program that is state administered. To check on your eligibility, go to http://familiesusa.org/.

- If you don't qualify for Medicaid, you may be able to get health coverage for your children through the federal State Children's Health Insurance Program (SCHIP). Go to www.insurekidsnow.gov for information about the program in your state.

Bring in More Bucks

If slashing your spending doesn't free up all the money you need to meet your financial obligations *and* accelerate the rate at which you pay off your debts, look for ways to increase your household's monthly income. Maybe you need to work extra hours at your current job (if you're paid by the hour), take a second job, or work as a freelancer.

If your spouse or partner is a stay-at-home parent and is considering getting a paying job, take into account the costs of working outside the home, such as childcare and transportation, so you can be sure that the change makes financial sense.

If making more money will be an uphill battle because demand for your skills is declining or because the industry you work in is depressed, consider getting trained for a new career by attending your local community college or a reputable trade school. Before you leap into anything, however, find out where the experts expect future job opportunities to be. Start your research by looking through the *Occupational Outlook Handbook,* a publication available at the website of the U.S. Department of Labor's Bureau of Labor Statistics, www.bls.gov.

Earn more at your current job

If you're paid by the hour, let your boss know that you want to work additional hours. You may be able to add another shift to your schedule, work longer each day, or work on weekends, especially if you have a good reputation as an employee.

Asking for a raise is another option, assuming that you can justify your request. For example, a raise may be in order if you haven't received one in a long time, if you have assumed new responsibilities without additional compensation, or if you recently completed an important project.

_____

_____

_____

You can also apply for a promotion. Let your boss know that you want to be considered for a higher-paying job in your current department. If you're qualified to work in other departments, meet with those managers to let them know you're interested in working for them.

Look for a new job

Getting a better-paying job with a new employer is another obvious way to boost your income. This section shares tips for starting a job search.

Do your homework

Prepare for your job hunt by whipping your résumé into shape, writing a short but snappy cover letter, and honing your interview skills. If you need help doing any of these things, you'll find a wealth of free information on the web:

- **The career advice section of Monster.com:** At www.monster.com, you can find résumé assistance, help in figuring out how much salary to ask for, and a self-assessment center for evaluating your skills and abilities. You also get advice based on whether you want to change careers, are looking for a job, or are 50 years old or over.

- **CareerBuilder:** This website helps you build an online résumé from scratch or improve the one you already have. Then you can post it at the site for employers who are looking for someone like you. Go to www.careerbuilder.com.

Find out about new job opportunities

When your résumé and cover letter are up to date and you're ready to turn a practice interview into a real one, how do you find potential employers?

- **Let your friends know you're in the market for a better-paying job.** They can keep an eye out for opportunities at their workplaces.

- **Visit job search websites.** Scope out a variety of job sites to find ones that best meet your needs and are easiest to use. National online job websites include CareerBuilder (www.careerbuilder.com), Job-Hunt.org (www.job-hunt.org), Monster.com (www.monster.com), and CareerOneStop (www.careeronestop.org). Some of these sites send you email alerts to let you know about new job listings that match your criteria.

Niche online job sites focus on a narrowly defined type of job or on jobs within a specific industry. For example, `www.dice.com` focuses on high-tech jobs; `www.bankingboard.com` zeroes in on jobs in the mortgage banking, title, escrow, and real estate fields; and `www.allretailjobs.com` focuses on all types of positions in the retail world.

Most state employment office sites include a job bank of openings with local and national private-sector employers, nonprofits, state government, and sometimes local governments. The websites of your local and county government may feature job banks with a focus on government job openings in your specific locale.

Many professional or trade organizations list job openings of specific interest to their members.

Visit `www-cms.livecareer.com/quintessential/top-50-sites` for descriptions and links to 50 great job sites. You can also search for jobs by industry type — from jobs in the airline industry and law enforcement to jobs in academia, fashion, retail, finance, and advertising — at `www-cms.livecareer.com/quintessential/indres`.

- **Read the employment listings in your local newspapers.**

- **Attend job fairs.** Job fairs are a great way to meet employers in your area that are hiring. You may even have the opportunity to do some initial interviews at the job fairs or set up interviews for a later date. You can find out about job fairs through your local media; by visiting www.careerbuilder.com or other websites dedicated to job fairs; and by searching the Internet.

- **Network.** Many great jobs are never advertised online or in newspapers. Instead, they are filled via word of mouth, through networking. Networking involves letting anyone and everyone know that you're looking for a job, including your former bosses, professional associates, friends, relatives, neighbors, elected officials you may know, and even people you just happen to meet.

  You can also attend networking events. For example, your local Chamber of Commerce may sponsor breakfasts, luncheons, or happy hours that are organized to help professionals network. Other good networking opportunities include meetings of your alumni association, meetings of clubs and associations you may belong to, community events, cocktail parties and dinner parties, and conferences.

When you're networking, be prepared to explain in concise terms exactly what type of job you're looking for and your skills and experience. You may have only a minute to make a first impression. Carry business cards with you at all times to take full advantage of every networking opportunity that comes your way. And whenever you meet people who could be helpful in your job search, get their business cards so you can follow up.

- **Find a headhunter.** Schedule an appointment with an employment agency in your area or with an executive-recruitment firm (also known as a *headhunter*) if you're looking for a mid- to upper-level management position.

Employment agencies and executive-recruitment firms are paid a fee for linking up employers and employees. Typically, employers pay the fees of executive-search firms, but you may have to pay the fee if an employment agency finds you a job. Be clear about who will pay before you sign an agreement with a business that says it will try to help you find employment. If you'll be responsible for the fee, make sure you understand the amount and the conditions of the fee you'll owe.

Get (and survive) a second job

Thinking about making more money by working at another job, also known as *moonlighting?* Moonlighting can be a great way to make extra bucks, as long as your second job doesn't interfere with your ability to be effective at your primary job. You also need to make sure you come out ahead financially after taking into account any additional expenses you may incur by working two jobs: transportation, childcare, and so on.

If you signed a contract with your current employer, read it before you take a second job. The contract may prohibit you from working for specific types of employers or from moonlighting at all.

If you feel like your life is already a juggling act, a second job will make keeping all your balls in the air even more

_____

_____

_____

of a challenge. However, you can take steps to alleviate some of the stress that working multiple jobs may create:

- Ask your spouse or partner and older children to assume more day-to-day chores.

- Create a schedule of when things need to be done and post it on your family's bulletin board or refrigerator.

- Accept the fact that, for now, some things at home will fall through the cracks, and everything may not get done according to your standards.

- Make nutritious one-pot meals that you can freeze and that will feed your family for several days.

- Try to find a second job you enjoy — maybe relating to a hobby or special interest.

- Avoid taking a second job that involves a lot of pressure and stress, especially if you're already under a lot of pressure and stress at your main job.

- Look for a second job that is relatively close to either your home or your main job so you're not spending a lot of time commuting.

- Grab naps when you can.

Consider freelancing

Depending on the skills you have, you may be able to boost your income by doing part-time freelance work. When you're a freelancer, you are self-employed and offer your services to other businesses. For example, you may be a freelance copywriter, graphic designer, software designer, or CPA.

Working for yourself may sound appealing and can be quite profitable, but if you need an immediate infusion of cash, it's probably not your best bet. Usually, before you can expect to see any money from freelancing, you have to

- Prepare information explaining your services.

- Decide how and how much you will charge for services.

- Let potential clients know about your services and then hope that some of them will contract with you.

- Invoice your clients after you're hired and cross your fingers that they'll pay you quickly.

Obviously, being a successful freelancer, especially when you're holding down a regular job, takes organization, self-discipline, the ability to manage numerous tasks simultaneously, and a little bit of luck. However, if freelancing appeals to you, you can use these avenues to find out more:

- Talk to people you know who are already freelancing.

- Let former employers know you would like freelance work.

- Visit www-cms.livecareer.com/ quintessential/freelancing-career.

- Register at www.guru.com so that businesses looking for someone who offers your type of service can find you.

When you freelance, your clients won't deduct taxes from the money they pay you, so you owe those taxes to Uncle Sam on April 15. If you're making a considerable amount from freelancing, it's a good idea to pay your taxes quarterly. Otherwise, you may end up in hot water with the IRS if your tax return shows that you owe more taxes than you can afford to pay when April 15 comes around. Meet with your CPA to figure out the best way to handle your taxes as a freelancer.

6

Consolidating Your Debts

Debt consolidation is another option for managing your debts when you owe too much to your creditors. It involves using new debt to pay off existing debt. This chapter explains when debt consolidation is and isn't a good strategy. It also explains how different options work and reviews their pros and cons. You're then warned against dangerous debt-consolidation offers that harm your finances.

When Debt Consolidation Makes Sense

When you consolidate debt, you use credit to pay off multiple debts, exchanging multiple monthly payments to creditors for a single payment. When done right, debt consolidation can help you accelerate the rate at which you get out of debt, lower the amount of interest you have to pay to your creditors, and improve your credit rating. But to achieve these potential benefits, the following criteria need to apply:

- **The interest rate on the new debt is lower than the rates on the debts you consolidate.** Say you have debt on credit cards with interest rates of 22 percent, 20 percent, and 18 percent. If you transfer the debt to a card with a rate of 15 percent, you improve your situation.

- **You lower the total amount of money you have to pay on your debts each month.**

- **You don't trade fixed-rate debt for variable-rate debt.** The risk you take with a variable rate is that although the rate starts out low, it could move up.

- **You pay off the new debt as quickly as you can.** You apply all the money you save by consolidating (and more, if possible) to pay off the new debt.

- **You commit to not taking on any additional debt until you pay off the debt you consolidated.**

Another advantage of debt consolidation is that by juggling fewer payment due dates, you should be able to pay your bills on time more easily. On-time payments translate into fewer late fees and less damage to your credit history.

However, too many consumers consolidate their debts and then get deep in debt all over again because they are not good money managers, have spending problems, or feel less pressure after consolidation and get careless about their finances. For them, debt consolidation becomes a dangerous no-win habit.

Consider Your Options

You can consolidate your debts in several ways: transferring high-interest credit card debt to a credit card with a lower interest rate, getting a bank loan, borrowing against your whole life insurance policy, or borrowing from your retirement account.

Deciding whether debt consolidation is right for you and which option is best can be difficult. If you need help figuring out what to do, talk to your CPA or financial advisor, or get affordable advice from a reputable nonprofit credit-counseling organization (see Chapter 7). Otherwise, you may make an expensive mistake.

Transfer balances

Transferring high-interest credit card debt to a lower-interest credit card is an easy way to consolidate debt. You can make the transfer by using a lower-rate card that you already have, or you can use the web to shop for a new card with a more attractive balance transfer option. Sites to shop at include www. cardtrak.com and www.cardratings.com.

Before you transfer balances, read all the information provided by the card issuer that explains the terms and conditions of the transfer. You may conclude that the offer isn't as good as it appeared at first glance. For example, you may find that the transfer offer comes with a lot of expensive fees and penalties, and that the interest rate on the transferred debt can skyrocket if you're just one day late with a payment.

Also, higher interest rates (not the balance transfer interest rate) apply to new purchases you make with the card, as well as to cash advances you get from it. If the credit card offer does not spell out what the higher rates are, contact the card issuer.

When a credit card company mails you a pre-approved balance transfer offer, the interest rate on the offer may not apply to you. Most offers entitle the credit card company to increase the interest rate after reviewing your credit history.

To be sure that a balance transfer offer will really save you money, ask the following questions:

- **What's the interest rate on the offer, and how long will the rate last?** Many credit card companies try to entice you with a low-rate balance transfer offer, but the offered interest rate may expire after a couple of months, and then it may increase considerably. If you can't afford to pay off the new debt while the low-rate offer is in effect, don't make the transfer unless the higher rate will still be lower than the rates you are currently paying.

  Note: Some people try to avoid higher rates on transferred credit card debt by regularly moving the debt from one card to another. Doing so damages your credit history and hurts your credit scores.

- **What must I do to keep the interest rate low?** Know the rules. Usually, a low rate will escalate if you don't make your card payments on time. However, if the card you use to consolidate debt includes a *universal default clause,* the credit card company can raise your interest rate anytime if it reviews your credit history and notices that you were late with a payment to another creditor, took on a lot of new debt, bounced a check, and so on.

The method you use to transfer credit card debt — going to the bank to get a cash advance through your credit card, writing a convenience check, or handling the transfer by phone or at the website of the credit card company — can affect the interest rate you end up paying on the new debt, as well as the fees charged as a result of the transfer. Typically, getting a cash advance at your bank is the most costly option. Before you transfer credit card debt, know the interest rate and fees associated with each transfer option; choose the one that costs the least.

If you decide to use a convenience check from a credit card company, be aware that some checks may have lower interest rates than others, and the interest rates associated with some checks may last longer than with others. The company should spell out the terms associated with each check in the information it mails with the checks. If you're confused, call the company.

- **When will interest begin to accrue on the debt I transfer?** Usually, the answer is "right away."

- **How much is the balance transfer fee?** Fees vary, but typically they are a percentage of the amount you transfer, although some credit card companies may cap the amount of the fee at $50 to $75. Some credit card companies charge a flat balance-transfer fee.

- **What method will the credit card company use to compute my monthly payments?** Credit card companies use one of several types of balance-computation methods to determine the amount you must pay each month; some methods cost you more than others. Look for a card that uses the *adjusted balance* or the *average daily balance (excluding new purchases)* method to figure out your minimum monthly payments. Avoid credit cards that use the *two-cycle average daily balance* method, if you can.

Also note whether the card has a 20-, 25-, or 30-day *grace period* — the number of days between statements. You pay the most to use a card with a 20-day grace period.

_____

_____

_____

If you plan to make purchases with the credit card after you've paid off the transferred card balances, pay attention to the interest rate that applies to new purchases. Also, if you use the card to make purchases, the bank that issued the card will probably apply your payments to the lowest interest rate balance first. So every time you make a purchase, you're potentially converting lower-rate debt to higher-rate debt.

Get a bank loan

Borrowing money from a bank (or a savings and loan or credit union) is another way to consolidate debt. However, if your finances aren't in great shape, you may have a hard time qualifying for a loan with an attractive interest rate. You can use different types of loans to consolidate debt, as you see in the following sections.

 When you're in the market for any type of loan, it pays to shop around. However, if you have a good long-standing relationship with a bank, contact it first.

Take out a debt-consolidation loan

As the name implies, a debt-consolidation loan has the specific purpose of helping you pay off debt. Depending on the state of your finances and how much money you want to borrow, you may qualify for an *unsecured* debt-consolidation loan — one that doesn't require a lien on your assets.

If you qualify for only a *secured* debt-consolidation loan, you have to let the bank put a lien on one of your assets. That means that if you can't keep up with your loan payments, you risk losing the asset. If you have no assets to put up as collateral, a debt-consolidation loan is out of the question.

Think twice if a lender tells you that the only way you can qualify for a debt-consolidation loan is to have a friend or family member cosign the note. As cosigner, that person will be as obligated as you are to repay the debt. If you can't keep up with your payments, the lender will expect your cosigner to finish paying off the note, and your relationship with the cosigner may be ruined as a result. Plus, making the payments could be a real financial hardship for your cosigner, and if she falls behind on them, her credit history could be damaged.

Borrow against your home equity

If you're a homeowner and current on your mortgage payments, some lenders may suggest that you consolidate your debts by borrowing against your home's equity. *Equity* is the difference between your home's current value and the amount of money you still owe on it. Most lenders will loan you up to 80 percent of the equity in your home, as long as it's your primary residence, less if not.

 Some lenders let you borrow more than the value of your equity. Never do that. If you borrow more than the value of your equity and then you need or want to move, you can't sell your home because you owe more on it than it is worth.

Consolidating debt by using a home equity loan can be attractive for a couple of reasons:

- It's a relatively easy way to pay off debt, and the loan's interest rate is lower than in some other debt-consolidation options.

- Assuming that you're not borrowing more than $100,000, the interest you pay on the loan is tax deductible.

However, your home secures the loan, which means that if you can't make the loan payments, *you can lose your home.* If your finances are going down the tubes, borrowing against the equity in your home is risky business. And even if you're able to meet your financial obligations right now, if you owe a lot to your creditors and you have little or nothing in savings, a job loss, an expensive illness, or some other financial setback could make you fall behind on your home equity loan.

Also, be aware that if you sell your home and you still owe money on your mortgage and your home equity loan, you have to pay back both loans for the sale to be complete. If your home doesn't sell for enough to pay off everything you owe, you have to come up with the money to pay the difference. If the housing market in your area is cooling, and especially if you paid top dollar for your home, consolidating debt by tapping your home's equity is probably not a good move.

If you do decide that a home equity loan makes sense for you, keep the following in mind:

- Borrow as little as possible, not necessarily the total amount that the lender says you can borrow.

- Pay off the debt as quickly as you can. Lenders typically offer very relaxed home equity loan-repayment terms, and why not? The longer it takes you to repay your home equity debt, the more money the lender earns in interest.

- Know your rights. When you borrow against your home, the Federal Truth in Lending Act requires lenders to give you a three-day cooling-off period after you sign the loan paperwork. During this time, you can cancel the loan in writing. If you do, the lender must cancel its lien on your home and refund all the fees you've paid.

- Beware of predatory home equity lenders who encourage you to lie on your loan application so you can borrow more money than you actually qualify for. These lenders gamble that you'll default on the loan and they'll end up with your home. The same is true of unscrupulous home equity lenders who *overappraise* your home (give it a greater value than it's really worth) in order to lend you more money than you can afford to repay.

- Steer clear of lenders who want you to sign loan agreements before all the terms of the loan are spelled out, and avoid loans with prepayment penalties.

You can tap the equity in your home in one of two ways:

- **Home equity loan:** The loan has a fixed or variable interest rate, and you repay it by making regular monthly payments for a set amount of money over a specific period of time. If you apply for a variable-rate loan, be sure you understand what will trigger rate increases and the likely amount of each increase.

If you're not careful, the initial rate can increase so much that you may begin having problems making your loan payments.

- **Home equity line of credit (HELOC):** A *HELOC* functions a lot like a variable-rate credit card. You're approved to borrow up to a certain amount of money — your credit limit — and you can tap the credit when-ever you want, usually by writing a check. Typically, a lender will loan you up to 80 percent of the value of the equity you have in your home. The lender also reviews your credit history and/or credit score and takes a look at your overall financial condition.

  Although you have to repay a home equity loan by making fixed monthly payments that include both interest and principal, with a HELOC, you usually have the option of making interest-only payments each month or paying interest and principal on the debt. If you opt to make interest-only payments, the amount of the payments depends on the applicable interest rate and on how much of your total credit limit you are using. For example, if you have a $10,000 HELOC but you've borrowed only $5,000 of that money, the amount of interest is calculated on the $5,000.

The problem with making interest-only payments is that the longer the principal is unpaid, the more your HELOC costs you, especially if the interest rate starts to rise. Also, if your HELOC expires after a certain number of years and there is no provision for renewing it, the lender will probably want you to pay the total amount you still owe in a lump sum, also known as a *balloon payment*. If you can't afford to pay it, you may lose your home.

Federal law requires lenders to cap the interest rate they charge on a HELOC. Before you sign any HELOC-related paperwork, get clear on the cap that applies. Also find out whether you can convert the HELOC to a fixed interest rate and what terms and conditions apply if you do.

Refinance your mortgage and get cash out

If you're paying on your mortgage, refinancing the loan at a lower rate and borrowing extra money to pay off other debts may be another option to consider. (The new mortgage pays off your existing mortgage.) However, refinancing is a bad idea if

- **You've been paying on the mortgage for more than ten years, assuming it's a 30-year note.** During the first ten years of a loan, your payments mostly go toward the interest on your loan and only a relatively small amount of each of your payments is applied to your loan principal. However, after ten years of making payments, you begin whittling down the balance on your loan principal at a faster rate. This means that with each payment you are closer to having your mortgage paid off and to owning your home outright. If you refinance your loan, however, you start all over again with a brand-new mortgage, which means that you'll be paying mostly interest on the loan for a long time to come. Even so, if the new loan has a shorter term than your previous loan, paying mostly interest at first may not be an issue.

- **You can't afford the payments on the new loan.** If you fall behind, eventually your mortgage lender will initiate a foreclosure.

It may make sense to consolidate debt by going from a 30-year note to a 15-year note. (You pay less interest on a 15-year mortgage, so going from a 30-year to a 15-year loan won't double your monthly payments.) Run the numbers with your loan officer.

You're playing with fire if you use a mortgage refinance to consolidate debt by trading a traditional mortgage for an interest-only mortgage. Sure, your monthly payments may be lower initially, but after five years (or whenever the interest-only period ends), they will increase substantially, maybe far beyond what you can afford.

Borrow against your life insurance policy

If you have a whole life insurance policy, you can consolidate your debts by borrowing against the policy's cash value. If you have this kind of policy, you pay a set amount of money each month or year, and you earn interest on the policy's cash value.

This option has two advantages:

- You don't have to complete an application, and there's no credit check.

- After you borrow the money, you won't have to repay it according to a set schedule. In fact, you won't have to repay it at all.

But there's a catch, of course. After you die, the insurance company deducts the loan's outstanding balance from the policy proceeds. As a result, your beneficiary may end up with less than he or she was expecting, which can create a financial hardship for that person. For example, your surviving spouse or partner may need the money to help pay bills after your death, or your child may need the policy money to attend college.

Before you borrow against your life insurance, read your policy so that you understand all the loan terms and conditions. Also be clear about any fees you may have to pay because they will affect the loan's total cost. If you're unsure about anything, talk with your insurance agent or broker.

Borrow from your 401(k) retirement plan

If you're employed, you may be enrolled in a 401(k) retirement plan sponsored by your employer. If your employer is a non-profit, you may have a 403(b) retirement plan, which works like a 401(k). The money you deposit in your retirement plan is *tax-deferred* income; whatever you deposit in the account each year isn't recognized as income until you begin withdrawing it during your retirement years. Your employer may match a certain percentage of your deposits.

Most employers that offer 401(k) plans allow their employees to borrow the funds that are in their retirement accounts, up to $50,000 or 50 percent of the value of the account, whichever is less. If the value is less than $20,000, your plan may allow you to borrow as much as $10,000 even if that represents your plan's total value. No matter how much you borrow, you have five years to repay the money, and you're charged interest on the unpaid balance.

Borrowing against your 401(k) plan may seem like an attractive way to consolidate debt. However, unless you're absolutely sure that you can and will repay the loan within the required amount of time, taking money out of your retirement account to pay off debt is a *really* bad idea. Here's why:

- If you don't repay every penny within five years (and assuming that you're younger than 59½ when you borrow the money), you have to pay a 10 percent penalty on the unpaid balance. On top of that, the IRS treats whatever money you don't repay as an early withdrawal from your retirement account, so you're taxed on it as though it's earned income. On April 15, you can end up owing a whole lot more in taxes than you anticipated, and you may not have enough money to pay the taxes.

- You may promise yourself that you'll repay your retirement account loan, but with no lender (or debt collector) pressuring you into paying what you owe, are you disciplined enough to do that? If you're like a lot of consumers, you'll keep promising yourself that you'll pay back the loan, but you'll never get around to it. Or if you begin having trouble paying for essentials, those expenses will take priority, and you may have no money left to put toward repaying your retirement account loan.

- Every dollar you borrow represents one less dollar you'll have for your retirement if you don't repay the loan. Using your retirement account like a piggy bank could make your so-called golden years not so golden.

- While the loan is unpaid, your retirement account earns less tax-deferred interest. Therefore, the account will have less money when you retire.

- If your employer matches the contributions you make to your retirement plan, those contributions may end while you're repaying the loan. This also means less money for your retirement.

- Your employer may charge you a steep loan application fee — a couple hundred dollars or more. The fee increases the total cost of the loan.

- If you leave your job before you've paid off the loan — regardless of whether you leave because you found a better job, you were fired or laid off, or your employer went belly up — your employer will probably require that you repay the full amount of your outstanding loan balance within a very short period of time, somewhere between 30 and 90 days. If you can't come up with the bucks, the IRS will treat the unpaid money as an early withdrawal for tax purposes, and you'll also have to pay the 10 percent early withdrawal penalty.

Visit www.bankrate.com/calculators/ retirement/borrow-from-401k-calculator. aspx to figure out whether borrowing from your 401(k) is a good idea.

If you're younger than 59½, you may qualify for an early hardship withdrawal from your 401(k), even if your plan doesn't permit you to borrow from it. A withdrawal differs from a loan because you take the money out of your account without the option of repaying it. Therefore, you are permanently reducing the amount of money you'll have for your retirement. To be eligible for a hardship withdrawal, you must prove to your employer that you have "an immediate and heavy financial need" and that you've exhausted all other financial avenues for handling the need. Although your employer determines what constitutes this need, avoiding an eviction or foreclosure or paying steep medical bills almost certainly qualifies. You have to pay federal taxes on the money you take out for the year in which you get the money, and you also have to pay a 10 percent early withdrawal penalty.

Dangerous Debt-Consolidation Possibilities

When your debts are creating a lot of stress, your judgment may get clouded. You may start grasping at straws and do something really stupid that you would never do if you were thinking clearly — like fall for one of the many debt-consolidation offers out there that are outrageously expensive, and maybe even scams. Avoid some of the worst offenders:

- **Debt-counseling firms that promise to lend you money to help pay off your debts:** If you get a loan from one of these outfits, not only will it have a high interest rate, but you may also have to secure the loan with your home. In Chapter 7, discover how to find a reputable nonprofit counseling agency that can help you deal with your debts.

- **Finance company loans:** These companies often use advertising to make their debt-consolidation loans sound like the answer to your prayers. They are not. Finance company loans typically have high rates of interest and exorbitant fees. Working with a finance company will further damage your credit history.

- **Lenders who promise you a substantial loan, no questions asked, in exchange for your paying them a substantial upfront fee:** No reputable lender will make such a promise. Not only will these disreputable lenders charge you a high percentage rate on the borrowed money, but they will also put a lien on your home or on another asset you don't want to lose.

- **Companies that promise to negotiate a debt-consolidation loan for you and to use the proceeds to pay off your creditors:** In turn, they tell you to begin sending them money each month to repay the loan. The problem with many of these companies is that they never get you a loan or pay off your creditors. You send the company money every month while your credit history is being damaged even more, and you're being charged interest and late fees on your unpaid debts.

7

Negotiating with Creditors and Getting Help

If slashing your spending, making more money, and living on a strict budget don't resolve your financial problems, it's time to contact your creditors. This chapter tells you about the preparation you should do before you contact your creditors, and it fills you in on how to contact them and who to speak with. It also explains what you should say during your negotiations and highlights the importance of putting in writing the details of any agreement you may reach. You also find out what to do if you need help from a credit-counseling company.

Get Ready to Negotiate

Upfront planning and organizing is essential to the success of any negotiation. Your upfront planning and organizing should include

- Creating a detailed list of your debts
- Deciding which debts to negotiate first and what you want to ask from each of your creditors
- Reviewing your budget (see Chapter 4)
- Pulling together your financial information

If you don't feel comfortable about doing your own negotiating, you may want to ask your attorney or CPA to handle it for you, if you have a long-established relationship with that person. Assuming you have that kind of relationship, the CPA or attorney may agree to help you out for very little money. Another option is to get negotiating help from a nonprofit credit-counseling agency in your area (discussed later in this chapter). You can also ask a friend or relative for help, especially if you know someone who is good at making deals.

List all your debts

Create a list of all your debts, separating the ones that are high priority from the ones that are low priority. For each debt on your list, record the following information:

- The name of the creditor
- The amount you are supposed to pay every month
- The interest rate on the debt
- The debt's outstanding balance

Also, note whether you are current or behind on your payments. If you are behind, record the number of months you are in arrears and the total amount that is past due.

You should also note whether a debt is secured or unsecured. For each secured debt, write down the asset that secures it. For example, your house secures your mortgage and any home equity loans you may have. (Chapter 4 explains secured and unsecured debts.) When you list your unsecured debts, like your credit card debts and past-due medical bills, list them according to their interest rates. Put the debt with the highest rate at the top of the list, followed by the one with the next highest rate, and so on.

Leave space next to each debt on your list for recording the new payment amount you would like each creditor to agree to, or for recording any other changes you want from a creditor, such as a lower interest rate or the ability to make interest-only payments for a period of time. You will record this information after you have reviewed your budget.

Zero in on certain debts first

Some debts are more important than others because the consequences of falling behind on those obligations are a lot more severe. For example, if you don't keep up with your secured debts, the creditors may take back their *collateral:* the assets you used to guarantee payment. Negotiate these debts first:

- Your mortgage
- Your past-due rent
- Your car loan
- Your utility bills
- Your court-ordered child support obligation

- Your past-due federal taxes
- Your federal student loans

During your negotiations, don't be so eager to reach an agreement with a creditor that you offer to pay more than you really can afford. Also, don't agree to a temporary change in how you pay a debt if you really need the change to be permanent. If you can't live up to the agreement, most creditors probably won't negotiate with you again.

 When you negotiate your lower-priority debts, start by negotiating the one with the highest rate of interest.

Review your budget

After you create your list of debts, review your budget to figure out what you need from each creditor to be able to pay off any past-due amounts and keep up with future payments. For example, you may want a creditor to

- Lower the amount of your monthly payments on a permanent or temporary basis.
- Lower your interest rates.
- Let you make interest-only payments for a while.

- Waive or lower certain fees.
- Let you pay the amount that is past due by adding that total to the end of your loan rather than paying a portion of the past-due amount each month.

If you're at least 120 days past due on a debt, you may want to ask the creditor to let you settle the debt for less than the full amount you owe. The creditor may be willing to do that if it's convinced that settling is its best shot at getting some of what you owe. For example, the creditor may know that suing you for the full amount of your debt would be a waste of time because you are *judgment proof:* You have no assets that the creditor can take, and your state prohibits wage garnishment.

There can be federal tax ramifications to settling a debt for less than the original amount. The amount the creditor writes off is treated as income to you and may increase the amount you owe to the IRS when your taxes are due. For example, if you owe $10,000 to a creditor and the creditor agrees to let you settle the debt for $6,000, it sends the IRS a 1099 form reporting the $4,000 difference as income. However, you may not be affected if you are insolvent by IRS 1099 standards. A CPA can tell you whether the IRS considers you insolvent.

_____

_____

_____

When one of your creditors agrees to let you settle a debt for less, ask the creditor to report the debt as current and to remove all negative information related to the debt from your credit report. The creditor may or may not comply with your requests, but you won't know unless you ask.

Pull together your financial information

Some creditors may want to review your financial information before they agree to negotiate with you or agree to the changes you request. Gather the following information and put everything in one place for easy access:

- Your household budget
- The list of all your debts
- A list of your assets and their approximate values
- Copies of your loan agreements

Sharing information about your assets with creditors can be dangerous. If one of them decides to sue you to collect on your debt, you've made it easy for that creditor to figure out which asset(s) to go after. However, if you are anxious to strike deals with your creditors so you can continue paying off your debts, you are between a rock and a hard place; you may have no option but to share the information with them. Another risk you take by sharing information about your assets is that a creditor may demand that you sell one of your assets and give it the sale proceeds. However, you don't have to take that step unless you want to and unless doing so is in your best financial interest.

After you've pulled together your financial information, review your list of assets to determine whether you can use any of them as collateral. (Ordinarily, you must own the assets free and clear to use them as collateral.) Perhaps you own a motorcycle or RV, for example. As a condition of reaching an agreement, one of your secured creditors may require that you increase your collateral. If you do not have any assets to use as collateral, the creditors may decide it is too risky to work with you and take back the collateral you've already used to secure your debts with them.

A creditor may make a cosigner a condition of any new agreement. You should determine whether a friend or relative would be willing to cosign. As a cosigner, that person will be as responsible for living up to the agreement as you are, so if you default on the agreement, the creditor can look to your cosigner for payment. Before you ask someone to cosign, be sure that you can live up to the terms of the agreement. Also, make your friend or relative aware of the risks of cosigning.

Contact Creditors

After you've completed all your upfront planning and organizing, you're ready to contact your creditors. How you contact them — in person or by phone — and who you talk to depends on the type of creditor. For example, if the creditor is local (and not part of a national chain), an in-person meeting is appropriate, and you probably want to meet with the owner, credit manager, or office manager. However, if you want to negotiate your credit card bill, your mortgage, or the debt you owe to a national retail chain, for example, you start negotiating by calling the company's customer service number.

 If a creditor asks you to put your negotiating request in writing, send the details of your request via certified mail and request a return receipt. That way, you have confirmation that your letter was received, and you will know when to follow up.

Whenever you speak with someone, maintain a record of who you spoke to (name and title), the date of your conversation, what you asked for, how the creditor responded, and the specifics of any agreement. File away all sent or received correspondence related to your negotiations.

When you contact a creditor for the first time, explain that you are having financial problems and provide a general explanation of why the problems have occurred. For example:

- You lost your job.
- Your child is ill, and you have been saddled with a lot of unreimbursed medical expenses.
- You took on too much credit card debt.

Give the creditor confidence that you'll be able to live up to any agreement you may reach with each other by explaining what you are doing (or have already done) to improve your financial situation and to minimize the likelihood that you'll develop money problems in the future. For example:

_____

_____

_____

- You are living on a strict budget.
- You have enrolled in a money-management class.
- You are working at a second job.

Tell the creditor that you want to continue paying on your debt but you need the creditor to agree to some changes. Be specific about what you want the creditor to agree to. For example, you would like to pay $200 less each month on your debt.

 If you get nowhere with the first person you speak with, end your conversation and try negotiating with someone higher up, like a supervisor. That person is likely to have more decision-making authority and to be in a position to agree to your request. When you call a creditor for the first time, you may want to ask the person you speak with whether he has authority to negotiate with you. If not, ask who does.

Some of your creditors may refuse to negotiate directly with you and may indicate that you should contact a credit-counseling agency and let it do the negotiating for you. Later in this chapter, you find out how credit-counseling agencies work.

If the person you are negotiating with tries to pressure you into paying more than you can afford, stick to your guns.

Put an Agreement in Writing

Whenever you and a creditor reach an agreement, ask for the agreement to be put in writing. If the creditor refuses, prepare the agreement yourself, date and sign it, and then send a copy to the creditor. The agreement should include

- The duration.
- All deadlines.
- All payment amounts.
- Applicable interest rates.
- The amount of any fees you have agreed to and under what circumstance you must pay each fee.
- Everything the creditor has agreed to do or not do. For example, the creditor may agree to waive certain fees.
- When you and the creditor will be considered in default of the agreement and the consequences of the default.

If a problem develops with your agreement after it is official — if your creditor violates some aspect of the agreement or accuses you of doing the same thing — and you don't have the terms of the agreement in writing, resolving your differences may be difficult. Each of you is apt to have different memories of the agreement details. As a result, you may both have to hire attorneys to help you work out your disagreement, and you may end up in court where a judge will decide what to do.

Before you sign any agreement with a creditor, ask a consumer law attorney to review it. You want to be sure that you're adequately protected and that the agreement doesn't have the potential to create future problems for you.

Don't hire an attorney until you have found out how much he will charge to do the review, which should not take more than one hour of his time. Most attorneys charge between $100 and $500 per hour for their services, depending on where they practice law and the size of the law firms they work for: Attorneys in metropolitan areas on the East and West coasts tend to charge more than attorneys in rural areas or in the Midwest. Attorneys who work for large firms tend to charge more per hour than attorneys at smaller firms.

If you can't afford to hire an attorney, you may be able to get help from the Legal Aid Society in your area. Also, if a law school is in your area, it may run a legal clinic, and an attorney or law school student with the clinic can review your agreement for free. Another option is to contact your local or state bar association to find out whether it can refer you to a consumer law attorney who does a lot of pro bono work for financially strapped consumers.

After you have a final agreement with a creditor, revise your budget accordingly. When you are ready to contact another creditor, be sure that you prepare for your negotiations by working with the revised budget, not with your old one.

The Deal on Credit Counseling

Feeling overwhelmed by your debts and unsure how to take control of your finances, despite the advice you've read in this book? Have you tried without success to pursue options discussed elsewhere? There is a calm port in the storm called the *credit-counseling agency*. It can help you develop a budget and figure out a way to deal with your debts.

The benefits of credit counseling presume that you work with a reputable, nonprofit credit-counseling agency that employs trained, certified credit counselors and that charges fairly for its services. Many agencies talk a good game and have impressive websites, but they charge an arm and a leg for their services and deliver little in return. If you work with one of them, your finances could end up worse, not better.

If you're in the market for credit counseling, read on.

Find a Reputable Credit-Counseling Agency

A reputable agency evaluates your finances and comes up with a plan for helping you get out of debt and avoid financial problems in the future. Among other things, the agency

- **Reviews your budget to make sure it's realistic and suggests improvements and/or additional cuts.** If you do not have a budget, the agency helps you develop one.

- **Assesses the state of your finances.** After reviewing your financial information, the agency gives you a realistic picture of where you are right now financially: no better or worse off than a lot of consumers, on the brink of bankruptcy, or somewhere in between.

- **Figures out how you can keep up with your debts.** The agency may revise your budget to generate more *cash flow* (the amount of money you have to spend) each month to pay your debts off faster. Or it may recommend participating in a debt-management plan to lower your monthly debt payments to amounts you can afford. If your finances are in really bad shape, the agency may suggest meeting with a consumer bankruptcy attorney.

If the agency advises you to pay off your debts through a debt-management plan, the agency will explain how the plan works and review its pluses and minuses. Also, the agency should give you a general idea of how much you'll have to pay on your debts each month.

When a credit-counseling agency sets up a debt-management plan for you, the plan will address your *unsecured* debts, like credit card debts, unpaid medical bills, and student loans. Most credit-counseling agencies will not help you with your *secured* debts, such as your mortgage, home equity loan, and car loan.

- **Helps you set financial goals and provides you with financial education.** The financial education may include workshops, seminars, brochures, and workbooks.

_____

_____

_____

How to tell the good from the bad

Most counseling agencies are truly interested in helping consumers get a handle on their debts and develop a solid foundation for a financially sound future. However, some agencies are mostly out to make a buck (or lots of bucks) off consumers who are desperate for help and unaware of the differences between reputable and disreputable agencies.

Consumers who work with a bad-apple agency are apt to pay a lot of money — money they could have used to pay their debts or living expenses — and get little or nothing in return. Many of these consumers end up worse off financially than they were before. For example, bad-apple credit-counseling agencies may charge excessive fees, push consumers into debt-management plans when they don't need them (so the agencies can charge plan administration fees each month), and offer no financial education or goal-setting assistance.

That's the bad news. The good news is that it's relatively easy to find a good credit-counseling agency, assuming that you know the questions to ask and the telltale signs that an agency may not be on the up and up.

If an agency's promises about what it can do for you sound too good to be true, they probably are. No matter how much you may want to believe what it says, look for another credit-counseling agency to work with.

Avoid credit-counseling agencies that solicit your business by phone or email. Also, don't be impressed by agencies that spend money on glossy print ads and regular ads on TV or radio. Reputable organizations do not spend a lot of money on advertising and rely mostly on referrals and word of mouth.

How to locate agencies in your area

When you look for a credit-counseling agency to work with, check out a couple so you can feel confident that you are going to get good help. Ask friends or relatives who have had a good past experience with credit counseling for a referral. Don't know anyone who's worked with this kind of agency? Here are two other excellent resources for finding a good one:

- **The National Foundation for Credit Counseling:** www. nfcc.org or 800-388-2227

- **The Financial Counseling Association of America:** http://fcaa.org or 800-450-1794

The counselors who work for agencies that are affiliated with these two organizations are trained and certified.

Another excellent source of reputable credit-counseling agencies is the website of the United States Trustee. People who want to file for bankruptcy have to obtain a *certificate to file* from a credit-counseling agency. Only credit-counseling agencies that have been certified by the federal Trustee's office can issue this type of certificate. To find a certified credit-counseling agency in your state, go to www.justice.gov/ust and click on "Credit Counseling & Debtor Education."

If you don't find agencies in your area, or if you would have a difficult time going to an agency's office during business hours, many good agencies offer online counseling that can be just as effective as meeting face to face with a counselor.

What to ask and what to expect

After you have the names of some agencies, ask each the following set of questions by meeting with a representative from each agency, emailing them from their websites, or talking with them on the phone. Do not pay a credit-counseling agency any money or sign any paperwork until you have received satisfactory answers to each of these questions:

- **Are you a federally approved, nonprofit, tax-exempt credit-counseling agency?** Nonprofit agencies will charge you the least for their services and provide you with the most in return. Some credit-counseling organizations are for-profit businesses even though their names make them sound like they are nonprofits.

  Get proof that an agency is a nonprofit by asking for a copy of its IRS *approval of nonprofit status* letter. Don't work with an agency that refuses to let you look at this letter or never provides it.

- **Do you have a license to offer credit-counseling services in my state?** Although some states do not license credit-counseling organizations, many do. You can find out whether your state requires licensing by contacting your state attorney general's office. If your state does issue licenses, ask for the name of the licensing agency and then get in touch with it to confirm that the credit-counseling agency has a valid license.

_____

_____

_____

- **What services do you offer?** The upcoming section "Work with a Counselor" describes the services the agency should offer.

- **How do you charge for your services?** Reputable credit-counseling agencies charge little or nothing for most of their services. However, if you participate in a debt-management plan, you will be charged a small monthly administrative fee — probably $40 per month tops. Less-reputable agencies charge substantial upfront fees — as much as several hundred dollars — as well as steep monthly fees if they put you in a debt-management plan.

Some credit-counseling agencies that are not on the up and up don't charge large fees but charge a lot of small fees instead. Over time, all those small fees really add up. Ask the credit-counseling agency for a comprehensive list of fees. If it refuses to provide a list or tells you it does not have one, steer clear!

Some states regulate the amount of money a counseling agency can charge to set up a debt-management plan and to administer it. Contact your state attorney general's office to find out whether it regulates these fees.

Watch out for agencies that encourage you to give them voluntary contributions. The *contributions* are just fees to make the agencies more money at your expense.

- **Will I be assigned a specific credit counselor to work with?** You should expect to work with one counselor.

- **How do you pay your credit counselors?** Reputable agencies pay their counselors a salary or by the hour. Avoid agencies where the counselors make money by selling services. They are just commissioned salespeople who have a financial incentive to get you to buy as many services as possible whether you need them or not.

- **Can I see a copy of the contract I must sign if I work with you?** Don't work with an agency that does not use a contract or that won't share a copy with you. The contract should clearly state exactly what services the agency will be providing to you, a timeline for those services, and any fees or expenses you must pay. It should also provide information about any guarantees the agency is making to you, as well as the name of the credit counselor you'll be working with and the counselor's contact information.

- **How will you keep my personal and financial information private and secure?** With the rise of identity theft, the agency must have a strong policy in place to protect your information from strangers.

 Check out an agency with your local Better Business Bureau and with your state attorney general's office. If either organization indicates that numerous consumers have filed complaints against the agency, reconsider your decision.

You should also check with the Federal Trade Commission (FTC) at www.ftc.gov. The FTC is aggressively cracking down on businesses that pretend to be nonprofit counseling agencies.

Work with a Counselor

Your assigned credit counselor will become familiar with you and your finances. If you meet face-to-face with the counselor, you should expect your initial meeting to last about an hour, and you should expect to have a couple of follow-up meetings.

If you get your counseling online, you will exchange information and get your questions answered via email.

Share your financial situation

At your first meeting (or soon after), be prepared to provide your counselor with such information as the following:

- Your household budget, if you have one
- A list of your debts, including whether they are secured or unsecured
- The amount of money due on each debt every month
- The interest rate for each debt
- Which debts you are behind on
- The assets you own and their approximate *market values* (meaning how much you could sell them for)
- Copies of your most recent tax returns or pay stubs reflecting your monthly take-home pay

The counselor uses all this information to prepare a plan customized just for you. Not only will the plan provide you with a road map for getting out of debt, but it should also help you work toward financial goals like buying a home.

_____

_____

_____

As part of your plan, the credit counselor may suggest that you enroll in one or more of the agency's money-management seminars and workshops so you can gain the information and tools you need to avoid debt problems in the future and achieve your financial goals. Also, the counselor may give you free money-management materials to read.

Use a debt-management plan

If your counselor can't figure out a way for you to pay off your debts by reducing your expenses and maybe making more money, he may recommend participating in a debt-management plan. When you participate in such a plan, the counselor tries to negotiate smaller monthly payments with your creditors.

Get creditors to buy in

The counselor determines exactly how much you can afford to pay to your unsecured creditors each month in order to eliminate each debt over a three- to five-year period. Then he contacts the creditors to find out whether they will agree to let you pay the amounts you can afford. He may also ask for other concessions, such as lowering your interest rates.

If your unsecured creditors believe that giving you what you need is their best shot at getting the money you owe, and if they believe you are likely to file for bankruptcy otherwise (which means they may not get a penny from you), they will probably agree to the plan the credit counselor has proposed. However, most large creditors will have a minimum amount they expect you to pay on your debts each month; unless you commit to paying it, they won't agree to participate in your plan. If some creditors refuse to work with you, you have to continue paying them according to the original agreements.

Many creditors are willing to offer special concessions to consumers who pay off their debts through a debt-management plan. In return, they expect that consumers will not incur additional debt while they are in their plans.

Work the plan

After the counselor has prepared your final debt-management plan, ask for a copy. Do not sign it until you have read it carefully, understand everything in it, and are sure that you can live up to it. Note any restrictions. For example, it may prohibit you from taking on additional credit with your current creditors. If you violate any aspect of your plan, you risk having it canceled.

When your plan is official, you pay your counselor every month the amount of money you have agreed to pay on your debts, as well as the required monthly fee. In turn, the counselor pays your creditors. Make sure your plan says that your counselor will send you regular monthly updates on the status of your plan.

Beware of agencies that spend little or no time evaluating your finances before advising you to enroll in a debt-management plan or that ask you to begin paying on a plan before your creditors have agreed to work with you.

Also, be aware that some creditors who agree to be part of your plan may report you as slow paying or as paying through a debt-management plan, which will damage your credit history a little. However, statistics show that successfully completing a debt-management plan actually increases your *FICO score* — the numeric representation of your creditworthiness that is derived from the information in your credit history. (For more on FICO scores, see Chapter 1.)

Actively manage your plan

Even when you are careful about choosing a counseling agency to work with, if you participate in a debt-management plan, problems that may undermine the plan benefits can develop. These tips can minimize the potential for problems:

- After your counselor tells you which of your unsecured creditors have agreed to participate in your debt-management plan, contact them to confirm their participation before you send the counselor any money.

    However, taking this step before paying any money may not always be possible. Due to cost constraints, a nonprofit credit-counseling agency may not contact your creditors to find out whether they will participate in your debt-management plan until you have given the agency an initial month's payment on the plan. The agency wants to be sure that you are serious about paying your debts before it spends time negotiating the plan details with creditors.

- If your counselor tells you that one of your creditors won't agree to participate in your plan until you send the counselor an upfront payment, contact the creditor to confirm that what the counselor says is true.

- Make sure that the schedule your counselor sets up for paying your debts provides enough time for your creditors to receive what they are owed each month before the payment due dates. Otherwise, you risk racking up late fees and penalties.

- Every month, just after the date that your counselor is due to make a payment, confirm with the counselor that the payment was made on time.

- Whenever you receive a monthly statement of your account from one of the creditors participating in your debt-management plan, review it carefully to make sure your account was credited appropriately. Also, make sure that each creditor made whatever concessions it agreed to make, such as lowering your interest rate, waiving certain fees, or allowing you to make reduced payments or interest-only payments for a while.

Avoid Debt-Settlement Firms

Some people confuse debt-settlement firms, also known as *debt-negotiation firms,* with credit-counseling agencies. The services they offer are very different from those of a legitimate counseling agency. Also, if you work with a debt-settlement firm, you risk harming your finances and damaging your credit history and FICO score.

Be wary of false promises

Debt-settlement firms claim that they can settle your unsecured debts for less than the full amount you owe on them. They also claim that, after you pay the settlement amounts, your creditors will consider the debts paid in full. For example, if you owe $10,000 in credit card debt, a debt-settlement firm may tell you it can get the creditor to let you pay the debt off for $6,000.

You can try to settle your own debts for free (see the first half of this chapter). You don't need a debt-settlement firm to do it for you. But keep in mind, as mentioned in the earlier section "Review your budget," that if a creditor agrees to forgive part of your debt, the IRS will probably treat that forgiven amount as income to you, and you will be taxed on it. If you receive an IRS 1099 form related to a debt that you settled, talk to a CPA. If the CPA can prove that you were insolvent at the time that the amount of the debt was forgiven, you won't be taxed on that amount. You're *insolvent* if you don't have enough money to pay your debts and living expenses and you don't have any assets you can sell to pay off the debts.

Some debt-settlement firms also promise that after they settle your debts, they can get all the negative information related to those debts removed from your credit history. Not true — only the creditors that reported the negative information can remove it.

If you agree to work with a debt-settlement firm, you may be told to stop paying your unsecured creditors and to begin sending that money to the firm itself. The problem is that a debt-settlement firm may be all talk and no action. It may not be able to settle your debts for less. In fact, it may not even try. Furthermore, if it does intend to try to settle your debts, it may take months for the firm to accumulate enough money from the payments you are sending to be able to propose settlements to your creditors. Meanwhile, your debts are going unpaid, your credit history is being damaged further, and the total amount you owe to your creditors is increasing because late fees and interest are accumulating.

If you question a firm about the consequences of not paying your debts, you may hear that your unsecured creditors won't sue you for their money. That is flat-out wrong.

Prevent worse financial problems

Debt-settlement firms charge much more money than legitimate counseling agencies. If you work with a firm, you may have to pay one or more substantial upfront fees, as well as additional fees that may be based on the number of unsecured credit accounts you have, the amount of debt you owe, or the amount of debt that the firm gets your creditors to forgive. The cost of working with a firm may be more than the amount of money you save from settling your debts.

Be careful if a debt-settlement firm offers to loan you money. Not only is the loan likely to have a very high interest rate and other unattractive terms of credit, but if you are not careful, you may also sign paperwork giving the firm the right to put a lien on an asset you own. The firm is hoping that you'll fall behind on your loan payments so it can take the asset.

What to Do If You're Ripped Off

If you get taken by a disreputable counseling organization or by a debt-settlement firm, contact a consumer law attorney, who will advise you of your rights. He may recommend sending a letter on his law firm stationery to the counseling organization or debt-settlement firm threatening legal action unless amends are made (such as by giving your money back). The counseling organization or debt-settlement firm may agree to the attorney's demands in order to avoid a lawsuit. If it does not respond or refuses to do what the letter asks, you can decide whether you want to go forward with a lawsuit.

Assuming that you have a strong case, the attorney will probably represent you on a *contingent fee* basis. You won't have to pay the attorney any money to represent you. Instead, the attorney gambles that you will win your lawsuit, and he will take his fee from the money the court awards you as a result. If you lose your lawsuit, you do not have to pay the attorney a fee. However, depending on your agreement, win or lose, you may have to pay the attorney's court costs and any other fees and expenses related to your case.

Regardless of whether you sue the counseling organization or debt-settlement firm, file a complaint with your state attorney general's office, your local Better Business Bureau, and the Federal Trade Commission (FTC). Although these organizations can't help you get your money back or undo damage done to your credit history and FICO score, other consumers who may be thinking about working with the same counseling agency or debt-settlement firm may think twice after reading your complaint. Also, if your state attorney general's office or the FTC receives a lot of complaints about the agency or firm, it may take legal action. For example, it may file a class action lawsuit on behalf of everyone who was ripped off.

8

Considering Bankruptcy

Bankruptcy is shrouded in myth and prejudice. If you're like many folks, the first step on the road to financial recovery is overcoming your feelings of inadequacy, shame, guilt, and fear of the unknown.

This chapter encourages you to put aside myth and prejudice, and to look calmly at the advantages and disadvantages of bankruptcy. Only then can you make a rational decision about whether bankruptcy is the best choice for you and your loved ones.

Bankruptcy in a Historical Context

In the United States, the concept of bankruptcy is unique. Here, bankruptcy is viewed legally and perceptually as a means to an end, not *as* the end of a debtor's financial life. The Founding Fathers provided for bankruptcy in the Constitution. A series of laws passed (and sometimes repealed) by Congress during the 1800s shaped the American view of bankruptcy as not only a remedy for creditors but also a way to give honest yet unfortunate debtors financial rebirth. The Bankruptcy Act of 1898 established that debtors had a basic right to financial relief without creditor consent or court permission. American bankruptcy laws have come to be recognized as far more compassionate and much less punitive to debtors than the laws of other countries.

Like much of American law, the country's bankruptcy statutes reflect the constant tension between the competing interests of debtors and creditors. Think of it as a perpetual tug of war, with each side striving mightily but never pulling its opponent all the way over the line. To this day, the balance of influence between creditors and debtors is in an ever-present state of flux. Sometimes debtors have the upper hand. Other times, creditors get the edge.

The constant, however, is that Americans have always been (and remain) entitled to a fresh start. The obstacles you must clear to obtain this fresh start are not constant; they're always changing.

Modern-day bankruptcy is rooted in the Bankruptcy Code of 1978, a federal law that was produced after more than ten years of careful study by judges and scholars. More recently, creditors and their lobbyists essentially rewrote what was a pretty well-reasoned and fair law in their own image. The result was the Bankruptcy Abuse Prevention and Consumer Protection Act of 2005 — often known as the Bankruptcy Abuse Reform Fiasco, or BARF. It's not good for consumers. It's not good for the economy. It flies in the face of the risk/reward principles at the core of capitalism. And, in the long run, it's probably not even good for the credit industry, which wrote it.

So how did a one-sided, ill-considered bucket of BARF happen to pass both houses of Congress and presidential scrutiny? Some think the eight-year lobbying campaign by the credit card industry and the $100 million spent on campaign contributions may have had something to do with it.

Some speculate that lawmakers simply didn't pay a whole lot of attention to the fine print in an incredibly complex amendment that's about the size of a metropolitan telephone book.

Bankruptcy Myths

Bankruptcy is an economic decision, not a morality play, and you needn't be deceived into viewing it as anything else. The following sections look at some of the usual myths that are cast about by the credit industry.

"People who go bankrupt are sleazy deadbeats"

People file for bankruptcy because they're in debt. The more debt there is, the more bankruptcies there are. It really is that simple.

The credit industry stereotypes folks who file bankruptcy as worthless deadbeats taking advantage of a loophole-ridden legal system to dump their moral obligations on the backs of everyone else. This stereotype is false, discriminatory, and manifestly unfair. Sure, bankruptcies have increased dramatically along with consumer debt, although the number of bankruptcies per $100 million on consumer debt has remained remarkably constant. From the 1970s to the 1980s, filings virtually doubled. The pace continued to increase in the 1990s, with bankruptcy filings setting new records year after year, even with a seemingly robust economy and near full employment. In fact, by the mid-1990s, bankruptcy filings, on a per capita basis, were running some eight times ahead of filings during the Great Depression. About 1 out of every 75 households in America has a member who has filed bankruptcy.

As soon as BARF went into effect on October 17, 2005, the number of bankruptcies plummeted, yet the financial health of the middle class continued to deteriorate. This is explained by the following facts:

- Record numbers of people rushed to file bankruptcy before BARF went into effect.

- BARF made it more tedious and time-consuming to file bankruptcy.

- Because of the additional work involved, the fees attorneys charge for bankruptcy have doubled.

- Bill collectors have been lying to folks, telling them that they're not eligible to file under the new bankruptcy law.

But the days of declining bankruptcies are over, and the number of folks filing has been steadily increasing since BARF, and will continue to increase, especially as homeowners try to avoid foreclosure.

And who are these people filing for bankruptcy? Chances are they're your neighbors, regardless of what neighborhood you live in. Bankruptcy is an equal-opportunity phenomenon that strikes in every socioeconomic bracket.

The fastest-growing group of bankruptcy filers are older Americans. More than half of people 65 and older who are forced into bankruptcy are forced because of medical debts. Also, more families with children, single mothers, and single fathers are being driven into bankruptcy; the presence of children in a household triples the odds that the head of the household will end up in bankruptcy.

In any case, the image of the sleazy, deadbeat bankruptcy filer is a phantom and a scapegoat for irresponsible lending. The bankruptcy filer can be more accurately described as an ordinary, honest, hardworking, middle-class consumer who fell for aggressive and sophisticated credit marketing techniques, lost control, and unwittingly surrendered his financial soul to the devil that is debt.

"Bankruptcy is the easy way out for folks who can pay their bills"

Creditors have been making this claim since the 1800s, and it's as demonstrably wrong today as it was back then.

In recent years, the credit industry funded several *studies* — a handy euphemism for *propaganda,* the more accurate description — that supposedly support their argument that people are skipping to bankruptcy court to skip out of their obligations. Independent sources have debunked every one of these self-serving reports. Two financial arms of Congress, the General Accounting Office and the Congressional Budget Office, discredited several of these studies.

Bankruptcy isn't the cause of debt; it's the result. And it isn't the disease; it's the cure. Restricting access to bankruptcy court won't solve the problem of debt any more than closing the hospitals will cure a plague.

"Bankruptcy threatens the ethical foundations of our society"

Credit card companies furiously push plastic on virtually anyone willing to take it. At present, more than 1 billion credit cards are in circulation —about 10 for every household in the United States. Lenders mail out billions of credit card solicitations every year. Low- and moderate-income households, high school students, and the mentally disabled — or, in their vernacular, *emerging markets* — are popular targets of lenders.

According to the Administrative Office of the United States Courts, consumers between the ages of 18 and 25 are one of the largest-growing segments (next to seniors) of bankruptcy filers — students and other young people who lack the maturity and resources to handle debt.

Anyone can figure out that extending credit to folks with no income, no assets, and no track record is kind of dumb (not to mention morally questionable). But creditors are more than willing to ignore the dangers of tomorrow so that they can reap exorbitant interest rates today. They're counting on — literally banking on — your ignorance of the situation. They encourage robbing Peter to pay Paul by using credit card advances to pay off credit card bills. They convince many middle-class consumers to bleed all the equity out of their homes through aggressively marketed home equity loans — with much of it going to finance consumable products (mall junk) instead of the homestead of the American Dream. That hundreds of solid, middle-class folks find themselves in bankruptcy court isn't surprising.

But why, in the face of increasing credit card losses, does the credit industry continue to dispense credit with utterly reckless abandon? The answer is simple: It's profitable — extremely profitable, or least it used to be.

During the decade prior to BARF, bankruptcy filings increased 17 percent, while credit card profits soared 163 percent. But, as mortgage lenders are coming to learn, the chickens ultimately come home to roost. It remains to be seen how long it will take for credit card lenders to wake to the fact that they will likely suffer catastrophic losses even greater than those that now plague the mortgage lending industry.

"Honest folks pay a 'tax' to support people who are bankrupt"

Claiming that honest taxpayers are supporting people who are bankrupt is nothing short of an outright, bald-faced lie. The theory, trumpeted in press releases, is that hundreds of thousands of Americans routinely ignore their obligations, intentionally or recklessly drive up their debts, and then declare themselves insolvent, stiffing creditors and, ultimately, every bill-paying, hardworking, patriotic American.

Creditors note that they write off billions every year. Thus, the reasoning goes, if access to bankruptcy were restricted, the credit industry wouldn't suffer losses that it must pass along to consumers. So, they say, BARF is good for consumers.

They're not saying that they'll pass along any savings to their customers, though, and historically that has not been their practice. Besides, do you really believe that the credit industry paid politicians tens of millions of dollars to enact BARF in order to save you money? Not likely.

What You Can Gain Through Bankruptcy

If you have no way to pay your bills, you certainly need to consider bankruptcy. If you have an income but cannot repay your debts in full within three years while maintaining a reasonable standard of living, bankruptcy may be a wise option.

Bankruptcy isn't the solution when your motive is anything other than reasonable relief from your debts. The U.S. Bankruptcy Code was established to assist *honest debtors*, not to provide a haven for chiselers and charlatans. If your aim is to jerk some creditor around, weasel out of debts you can easily pay, evade child support, or generally just stiff someone, bankruptcy is the wrong route. No one should use bankruptcy for vengeance or as a stopgap measure, or as a ploy or a bargaining chip. Don't file bankruptcy unless you're serious about following through.

Bankruptcy can

- Halt almost every kind of lawsuit.
- Prevent garnishment of any wages you earn after filing.
- Stop most evictions if bankruptcy is filed before a state court enters a judgment for possession.
- Avert repossessions.
- Stop foreclosures.
- Prevent your driver's license from being yanked for unpaid fines or judgments. (The stay doesn't prevent revocation or suspension of your driver's license for failing to pay court-ordered support.)
- Bring IRS seizures to a skidding stop.

Bankruptcy generally *doesn't* prevent

- Criminal prosecutions.
- Proceedings against someone who cosigned your loan, unless you file a Chapter 13 repayment plan and propose paying the loan in full.
- Contempt of court hearings.
- Actions to collect back child support or alimony, unless you file Chapter 13 and propose to pay off that obligation during the life of your plan.
- Governmental regulatory proceedings.

In recent years, some self-proclaimed "mortgage consultants" and "foreclosure service" outfits have made a business out of essentially tricking their clients into filing bankruptcy. These con artists exploit the bankruptcy laws to delay foreclosure, collect rents from the property during the delay, and then head for the hills. In the end, unsuspecting clients usually lose their homes and wind up with a bankruptcy on their records without realizing they'd even filed for bankruptcy. Bottom line: Discuss your options with an experienced bankruptcy attorney, not some fly-by-night flimflam operation.

Stop creditors in their tracks

The moment that you file a bankruptcy petition, a legal shield called the *automatic stay* kicks in, prohibiting creditors from contacting you, suing you, repossessing your property, or garnishing your wages.

After you file, a creditor can ask for permission to proceed with a repossession or foreclosure. But the creditor must obtain permission in advance, and the bankruptcy court judge may well turn down the creditor, if you propose a reasonable plan for paying that particular debt. (The following sections cover filing bankruptcy to eliminate some bills and pay others.)

Whenever a creditor is foolish enough to ignore the automatic stay, he'll have a federal judge on his back and may get zapped with a fine and an order to pay your attorney fees.

Wipe out most of your debts

Bankruptcy wipes out or *discharges* most debts. Credit cards, medical bills, phone charges, loans, and judgments all are usually *dischargeable*. However, some obligations generally are not eliminated in bankruptcy. These *nondischargeable* debts include the following:

- Student loans
- Alimony and child support
- Damages for a personal injury you caused while driving illegally under the influence of drugs or alcohol
- Debts from fraud
- Financial obligations imposed as part of a criminal conviction
- Taxes arising during the past three years

Catch up on back mortgage and car payments

Sometimes even dischargeable debts continue to haunt you when they're tied to one of your essential possessions. For example, you can wipe out loans secured by your home or car, but the creditor can still foreclose on your house or repossess your vehicle if you don't pay.

In a Chapter 13 bankruptcy (one in which you pay what you can toward your debts and the remainder is forgiven), you can propose a partial-repayment plan to avoid foreclosure and make up back mortgage payments over a five-year span. You can prevent repossession of your car by catching up on back payments of the life of the plan. In some situations, you have to pay only what the vehicle is worth instead of the whole loan balance.

File bankruptcy to pay some debts over time

Although some debts are not dischargeable, filing a Chapter 13 reorganization enables you to pay debts such as support obligations or back taxes over a five-year period and protects you from being hassled while you're paying down the balances. You can also gradually catch up on missed mortgage payments. In the meantime, most of your other debts are eliminated while you just pay for current expenses and keep current on future house and car payments.

Use bankruptcy to pay all your debts

Sometimes filing bankruptcy actually provides a way of paying all your debts instead of escaping them.

If the value of your property is sufficient to pay all your debts if only you had enough time to sell your assets, you can use bankruptcy to hold aggressive lenders at bay until your property is sold for the benefit of all your creditors — and possibly producing a surplus for you.

Say, for example, that you own investment property worth $150,000, on which you have a mortgage of $100,000, and that you have other debts totaling $25,000.

If you can sell the property, you can pay off the mortgage and other debts and still have something left over for yourself. But if the mortgage holder forecloses, neither you nor your creditors will likely receive a cent. Although the property *is* put up for public auction in a foreclosure, bidders rarely show up, and the only bidder typically is the mortgage holder, which merely bids the amount that's owed on the mortgage. In other words, the mortgage company ends up owning the property without paying any cash. Filing bankruptcy interrupts the foreclosure so that the property can be sold for everyone's benefit.

What You Can Lose Through Bankruptcy

Although bankruptcy may be that miracle cure you sought for your financial woes, you may encounter some unpleasant side effects. Consider the disadvantages of filing bankruptcy:

- **You can lose assets.** Depending on how much your home is worth and where you live, it is possible, but unlikely, that you'll lose it by filing bankruptcy. In most bankruptcies, debtors don't have to give up any of their belongings, but . . .

- **Bankruptcy is a matter of public record.** As more records are stored on computers and accessible on the Internet, searching that data becomes easier for anyone who's interested. In other words, if your nosy neighbor wants to know whether you filed bankruptcy, how much you owe, and who you owe it to, the information may be just a few mouse clicks away.

- **Bankruptcy affects your credit rating.** Bankruptcy may have a negative effect on your credit rating, but that fact may well fall into the "So what?" category for you. Even with a bankruptcy on your record, your odds of obtaining credit are very good. With a little work and perseverance, you can reestablish credit almost immediately. Some credit card companies actually target folks right after bankruptcy because they know that these people are free of all their existing debts and probably won't be eligible to file another bankruptcy any time soon. For a few years after bankruptcy, you may have to pay higher interest rates on new credit, but this result will ease over time, even if your credit report still shows a bankruptcy. So don't pay too much attention to the horror stories bill collectors tell you about the disastrous effect bankruptcy has on your credit. Furthermore, credit card companies will probably cancel all your cards.

- **Friends and relatives can be forced to give back money or property.** If you repaid loans to friends or relatives or gave them anything within the past year, they can be forced to repay a trustee the money they received, if you don't know what to watch out for. You can usually avoid these kinds of problems by carefully timing your bankruptcy filing.

- **Bankruptcy can strain relations with loved ones, especially parents who were raised in a different era.**

- **A stigma may still be attached to filing bankruptcy.**
  This drawback is especially true in small communities,
  but it is much less likely to be a problem in cities, where
  newspapers rarely bother printing the names of non-
  business bankruptcies.

- **Bankruptcy may cause more problems than it solves
  when you've transferred assets to keep them away
  from creditors.**

- **You can suffer some discrimination.** Although governmental agencies and employers aren't supposed to dis-
  criminate against you for filing bankruptcy, they may
  still do so in a roundabout way. Prospective employers
  may also refuse to hire you, and landlords may refuse
  to rent to you.

Alternatives to Bankruptcy

Bankruptcy isn't for everyone, and sometimes better solutions
are available. If it appears that the negatives outweigh the

positives, another route may be your best choice. Depending on your situation, one of these options may be the best alternative:

- Selling assets to pay debts in full
- Negotiating with creditors to reduce your debts to a manageable level
- Restructuring your home mortgage
- Taking out a home equity loan
- Doing nothing if you have nothing, expect to acquire nothing, and don't care about your present or future credit rating

In any event, weigh your decision on a simple, rational scale. Ask yourself whether the benefits outweigh the drawbacks. Many people, ravaged by guilt and shame, think they need to fully exhaust every alternative before considering bankruptcy, including the following:

- Making payments that never reduce the principal balance owed
- Taking out second mortgages to pay credit card debts
- Borrowing against pensions
- Withdrawing funds from retirement accounts

- Obtaining loans from friends and relatives
- Taking second jobs

Think seriously about the strain your financial distress places on your health, marriage, and family. Granted, bankruptcy is a very serious step that you shouldn't take lightly, but that doesn't mean you have to wait until you've lost everything. Think of it in these terms: If you have some blocked arteries, it just may be smarter to have bypass surgery *before* you have a heart attack. The same is true of bankruptcy. Think of bankruptcy as preventive medicine.

The Different Types of Personal Bankruptcy

Consumer bankruptcies are covered mainly under two parts of the U.S. Bankruptcy Code:

- **Chapter 7 liquidation** enables you to eliminate most of your debts but may require you to forfeit some of your assets for distribution to creditors.

- **Chapter 13 reorganization** enables you to pay off all
  or a portion of your debts during a three- to five-year
  time span but doesn't require you to forfeit any of your
  belongings or assets to pay *unsecured debts* (debts that
  are not secured by property, such as your car or another
  valuable asset).

Likewise, other special kinds of bankruptcy exist.
Chapter 11 bankruptcy is available to individuals but primarily
applies to large business reorganizations. Chapter 12 bankruptcy, which is similar to Chapter 13 bankruptcy, addresses
the unique problems family farmers and family fishermen
face. As a practical matter, almost all consumer cases are covered under Chapter 7 or Chapter 13 of the code.

Liquidations (Chapter 7)

Chapter 7, commonly referred to as *straight bankruptcy*, is often
what people mean or think of when they use or hear the term
generically.

In its simplest form, Chapter 7 wipes out most of your debts;
in return, you may have to surrender some of your property.
Chapter 7 doesn't include a repayment plan. Your debts are
simply eliminated forever. You obviously can *voluntarily* pay

back your creditors if you suddenly strike it rich, but legally you don't owe a dime after your debt is discharged. Most property you receive after filing Chapter 7 doesn't become part of your bankruptcy, but a few exceptions exist. Income tax refunds for prebankruptcy tax years go to pay your debts, as do divorce property awards, inheritances, and life insurance that you become entitled to receive within 180 days of bankruptcy.

Theoretically, a debtor's assets can be seized and sold for the benefit of creditors. All nonexempt assets owned on the petition date are fair game. They can be sold, with the proceeds distributed to your creditors. But in practice, 96 percent of consumer bankruptcies are *no-asset cases,* meaning that no property is taken away from the debtor because it's all exempt or worth so little that it's not worth the trouble.

To qualify for Chapter 7, if you earn more than the median income for your state, you must pass a new *means test,* in which you show that you don't have enough income to pay a significant portion of your debts. Although the test is complicated, when all is said and done, just about everyone can pass. The toughest part is just assembling the information you have to provide.

Consumer reorganizations (Chapter 13)

Chapter 13 involves a repayment plan in which you pay all or part of your debts during a three- to five-year period. In a Chapter 13 bankruptcy, you propose a debt-repayment plan that requires court approval and thereafter keeps creditors at bay as long as you keep making payments. This plan can be a great relief when you're able to establish and live within the confines of a budget.

A budget plan that demands frugality to the point of misery is doomed to fail. One that is reasonable has a good chance of succeeding. The operative word, however, is *reasonable*.

Every Chapter 13 plan must pass two tests:

- The *best-interest test*, which mandates that unsecured creditors be paid at least as much as they would receive if you filed a Chapter 7 instead of a Chapter 13.

- The *best-efforts test*, which requires that you pay all your disposable income (the amount left over after paying reasonable living expenses) to the trustee for at least the first 36 months of your plan. If your monthly income is more than the median for your state, allowable expenses will be based on Internal Revenue Collection Financial

Standards, and the plan must run for five years. Otherwise, the amount of your payment will be based on your actual expenses, as long as they are reasonable.

When you're done, you're done. Most creditors have gotten all they're going to get. Life goes on.

The Consequences of Not Filing Bankruptcy

In the same way that filing bankruptcy can have negative consequences, *not* filing can also have negative consequences. If you're eligible for bankruptcy but opt against filing, creditors have a number of options they can pursue, depending on whether a particular debt is secured by your property.

Claims secured by your car

If your car secures a debt, the creditor can repossess the vehicle and sell it to cover the loan. The proceeds of a repossession sale usually aren't enough to pay the debt, so you'll lose the car and still have to pay the balance that you owe on it — the worst of both worlds.

Although the law requires a creditor to sell a car in a "commercially reasonable" manner, that doesn't necessarily mean that the creditor will receive nearly as much as you can by selling it yourself. Before allowing repossession, you may want to try selling the vehicle. Your chances of getting more money for the car are greater than the finance company's. If you and your lawyer agree that it's best to get rid of the car because you just can't afford it, you can voluntarily surrender it to the lender instead of waiting for them to repossess it. Despite what people may tell you, your credit report will not look that much better, but at least you'll avoid the hassle of finding your car gone when you come out of the supermarket, or the embarrassment of a tow truck showing up at your house.

Claims secured by your home

Mortgage companies can't simply boot you out of your home if you miss a few payments. They must first go through a foreclosure procedure to extinguish your ownership rights. Although not all foreclosures involve court proceedings, all do take time — at least three months, in most cases, and frequently much longer. You can continue to live on the property until the foreclosure is completed.

Student loans

Government agencies can *garnish* (siphon off) up to 10 percent of your disposable income without going to court. A garnishment is almost like a withholding tax — the money is gone from your paycheck before you ever see it. You also need to be aware that Congress canceled state statutes of limitations on student loans. In other words, you can't just wait it out. You must deal with student loans. They won't disappear on their own.

Support obligations

Although debtors' prisons are officially a thing of the past, a divorce court can still send you to jail for neglecting your support obligations, and some states have programs to revoke professional licenses — such as licenses for practical nurses, accountants, or cosmetologists — of people who haven't kept up with their support.

Fines and restitution

If you've been ordered to pay a fine or make restitution in connection with a criminal proceeding and don't pay, accommodations at the local jail may await you. Don't tempt the judge;

some of them don't need much tempting to have you hauled off in handcuffs.

Taxes

The IRS has truly scary powers to seize your bank account, your pension, real property, or even the shirt off your back. State taxing authorities also have similar special powers. In addition, your town or city, your student loan creditors, or your ex-spouse or kids may be able to grab your tax refund whenever you owe alimony or support.

Lawsuits

Creditors with other types of claims can't do much without first suing you and obtaining a judgment. To do this, they must serve you with legal documents and give you a chance to dispute the debt in court. If you don't respond, a default judgment can be entered against you. That means the ruling goes against you even though you never presented your case.

The Statute of Limitations

Most debts — student loans being the most notable exception — eventually evaporate simply through the passage of time. In most cases, the *statute of limitations* (the time period within which an action must be commenced) is six years or less. But whenever a judgment has been entered against you, it can be as long as 20 years.

Sometimes the statute of limitations (usually ten years) can make federal taxes disappear.

Relying on the statute of limitations is a tricky proposition. If a creditor does sue to collect before the statute expires, the debt technically does not go out of existence, but merely becomes uncollectible. If someone sues you on a debt barred by the statute of limitations, they can still win and get a judgment unless you raise the statute of limitations as a defense to the suit. And there are reports of scavengers who pay pennies for debts barred by the statute of limitations and then try to collect them.

Also, it's frequently tough to figure out when the statute of limitations clock began ticking. Sometimes just making partial payments or acknowledging a debt can start the time running all over again. And you don't want that to happen.

About the Authors

Steve Bucci, BA, MA helped build one of the nation's largest credit-counseling services, Money Management International (MMI). MMI (www.moneymanagement.org) is not only accredited by the Council on Accreditation but is also a member of both the Association of Independent Consumer Credit Counseling Agencies and the National Foundation for Consumer Credit — the umbrella associations for credit counseling nationwide. In addition, all of their counselors are certified — and trained to help you find the best way out of debt.

Mary Reed is a personal finance writer who has coauthored or ghostwritten numerous books on topics related to consumer money matters and legal rights. Mary has also written for the magazines *Good Housekeeping*, *Home Office Computing*, and *Small Business Computing*, and she has ghostwritten numerous articles that have appeared in national and local publications. She is the owner of Mary Reed Public Relations, an Austin, Texas–based firm that provides public relations services to a wide variety of clients, including authors, publishers, attorneys, financial planners, healthcare professionals, retailers, hotels, restaurants, and nonprofits. She received her MBA from Boston University and her BA from Trinity University in Washington, D.C.